New Vanguard • 138

US Nuclear Submarines: The Fast Attack

Jim Christley · Illustrated by Tony Bryan

First published in Great Britain in 2007 by Osprey Publishing,
PO Box 883, Oxford, OX1 9PL, UK
PO Box 3985, New York, NY 10185-3985, USA
Email: info@ospreypublishing.com

Osprey Publishing is part of the Osprey Group.

© 2007 Osprey Publishing Ltd.

Transferred to digital print on demand 2014.

First published 2007
4th impression 2010

Printed and bound by PrintOnDemand-Worldwide.com,
Peterborough, UK.

A CIP catalogue record for this book is available from the
British Library.

ISBN: 978 1 84603 168 7

Page layout by: Melissa Orrom Swan
Index by Alison Worthington
Typeset in Helvetica Neue and ITC New Baskerville
Originated by PPS Grasmere Ltd, Leeds, UK

The Woodland Trust
Osprey Publishing are supporting the Woodland Trust, the UK's
leading woodland conservation charity, by funding the
dedication of trees.

www.ospreypublishing.com

Author's note

Operational depths and speeds. The Navy has kept classified
the details of the nuclear propulsion plant technology mainly
for reasons of both national security and to limit the free
transfer of technology on which large amounts of time, energy,
and money have been spent. The speed and diving depths of
nuclear submarines also fall under this classification. The
numbers stated below can be referenced in general
publications and do not constitute official values.

Nautilus	Surface speed/submerged speed: 22/23 knots Test depth: 700ft
Skate	Surface speed/submerged speed: 15/18 knots Test depth: 700ft
Skipjack	Surface speed/submerged speed: 15/29 knots Test depth: 700ft
Permit	Surface speed/submerged peed: 15/28 knots Test Depth: 1,300ft
Sturgeon	Surface speed/submerged Speed: 15/25 knots Test depth: 1,300 feet
Los Angeles	Surface speed/submerged speed: 15/30 knots Test depth: greater than 800ft
Seawolf	Surface speed/submerged speed: 15/30 knots Test depth: greater than 800ft
Virginia	Surface speed/submerged speed: 15/30 knots Test depth: greater than 800ft

Explanatory note

For the purposes of this text, unless otherwise stated, the term
"nuclear" refers to the nuclear reactor as a part of the
propulsion plant, not nuclear weapons.

Unless otherwise stated, all photographs are courtesy of the
US Navy.

Imperial/metric conversions

1 nautical mile – 1.85km
1 mile – 1.6km
1 yard – 0.91m
1ft – 0.3m
1in. – 2.54cm
1lb – 0.45kg
1 shaft horsepower – 0.735kW

Abbreviations

ADCAP	Advanced Capability
CCS	Combat Control System
ESM	Electronic Surveillance Measures
FY	Fiscal Year
shp	Shaft Horsepower
SRP	Submarine Recycling Program
SubRoc	Submarine Rocket
VLS	Vertical Launch System

US NUCLEAR SUBMARINES: THE FAST ATTACK

INTRODUCTION

This book constitutes a brief overview of the development of one type of submarine over a period of 50 years. Much of the history of these boats is shrouded in secrecy, and consists of thousands of men spending endless days on patrol, preserving the peace by their presence. In the main, they were and continue to be successful in this mission. Here is not a story of heroic battles where ships are torpedoed and aircraft shot down, but rather a story of engineering trade-offs and technological advances. The heroics are in the work itself.

THE PROPULSION PROBLEM

Early submarine evolution is marked by a struggle to overcome the problem of how to propel the submarine efficiently both on the surface and submerged. This engineering challenge can be divided into two interrelated concerns – hull form and propulsion. The propulsion problem drives the hull form problem.

The US submarine of 1945, embodied by the Balao and Tench classes, suffered from two serious shortcomings – limited underwater range and inadequate speed. To run completely submerged the submarine had to operate on its battery/electric motor combination alone. The range in

Polar bears examine a Sturgeon Class boat surfaced in the Arctic. When surfaced in the ocean for a swim call, the boat crew posts an armed shark watch. When surfaced in the Arctic, the boat has a polar bear watch. Even though the person is armed, his main job is not to kill the bears but to warn personnel on the ice that a bear has been sighted. On the occasion of a sighting the ice is evacuated, leaving the bear in charge of the territory.

this mode was 10 nautical miles (nm) at 8 knots or 50nm at 2 knots, the difference due to the batteries' ability to supply a large quantity of amps (high discharge rate) for a short time before they were exhausted and had to be recharged. A smaller discharge rate meant the boat moved slower but could do so for a longer time. An answer to this range endurance problem was the snorkel, a small induction pipe that reached above the surface and supplied air to the diesel engines, allowing them to run while the boat was submerged. However, the snorkeling submarine is noisier by far than one running on the same number of engines on the surface, and quietness is part of the submarine's underwater advantage.

The speed issue involved a rethinking of the entire outer shell (hull) design. A first step was to remove all the things that caused flow resistance, thus wasting energy. This modification cut the flow resistance of the World War II fleet submarine by nearly 50 percent, and was one of the principal measures of the Guppy conversion of many World War II boats. (Guppy was the Greater Underwater Propulsion Program, which extended the useful postwar life of diesel-electric submarines by removing items such as deck guns so as to streamline their hulls, increasing battery capacity, and the addition of snorkel systems.) For a given hull design, however, an increase in speed is directly dependent on the amount of power put into the water, and equates directly to shaft horsepower (shp). Speed is related to a change in shp as the cubic function of the change. Thus to go from 5 to 10 knots (doubling) requires an eightfold (two cubed) increase in shp. To go from the maximum 10 knots short-term submerged speed of a fleet submarine to the expected short-term speed of 15 to 20 knots of a replacement design required an increase from 5,400shp to over 18,000shp. Motor and battery designs capable of this horsepower would be huge and much too large for submarine requirements. Something else had to take the place of the diesel-electric design. Fortunately, a new source of energy was becoming available that would change everything.

From left to right: a Skate Class, a Permit Class, and a Tang Class. The two outboard boats are nuclear. The inboard boat is a diesel-electric. The fin-like protrusion on the bow of the Tang Class boat is the forward hydrophone set for the BQG-4 PUFFS sonar system, which became the Wide Aperture Array portion of the BQQ-5 on the Seawolf and Virginia Classes.

EVOLUTION – NAUTILUS TO VIRGINIA

The post-World War II US submarine community was faced with two significant challenges. First was a surplus of submarines that were of a ten-year-old design. The world for which they were designed effectively ceased to exist in late 1945 – it was perceived by the general public and many in the government that there was no threat on the horizon that required a large maritime presence. These boats and the strategy that surrounded their use had been premised on cutting enemies' lines of seaborne supply and communication. The submarine force had to find new tasks to support its continued existence. The second problem was the possibility that the Soviet Union possessed at least a dozen German Type XXI submarines and would reproduce this design or an improved design in large quantities. These boats were a distinct threat to the US Navy. Properly operated they were faster than destroyer sonar could track and could outrun a destroyer in rough seas. Thus any battle group that hoped to oppose a rapid Soviet advance into the North Atlantic or North Pacific oceans was seriously at risk.

To consider the options available for new submarines, the Office of the Chief of Naval Operations (OpNav) formed the Ship Characteristic Board (SCB) to replace the General Board for ship design. The SCB produced design requirements called characteristics and each was given a number. In addition, the SCB produced design policy documents that served as guidance for not only the design, but the fleet implementation of the design features. The SCB in 1945/46 realized that it had to redesign the fleet submarine and the new design had to be as good as, or (preferably) better than, the Type XXI U-boat. Design characteristics that the SCB wanted improved included sonar, weaponry, silencing, batteries and underwater endurance, propulsion systems, and underwater speed and control.

In the fall of 1945 Commodore Comstock, the head of the Bureau of Ships (BuShips), asked skippers and operational commanders for their views on new submarine design requirements in the areas of speed, design depth, power plants, and the effect of nuclear weapons on submarine operations and strategy. Based on the results, the design operating depth of new submarines was to be increased to 700ft, with an eye toward 1,000ft. Underwater speed would have to be increased – much of this could be attained by removing all external appendages, smoothing the hull lines, and through fairing. Model testing showed that a short submarine had better underwater performance than longer submarines.

The outcome of the initial design study was the 1947 design for the Tang Class (SCB 2). In addition to this design, in 1946 OpNav authorized an immediate experimental program that included two nuclear propulsion prototypes, four closed-cycle systems (in which the fuel and oxdizer carried onboard allowed the engines or boilers to be operated without external air), one arctic, and one midget submarine. This program was in addition to the build cycle for the Tangs. Budget restraints, however, limited the Tang schedule from six per year to two per year and put construction of the prototypes on hold because the designs were changing too fast. Then in 1950, the entire US defense budget was seriously curtailed. The submarine force struggled to have any new submarines built at all. By the time the Fiscal Year (FY) 1952

Down the hatch. Once a submarine is built everything that goes into the ship or comes out must pass through this vertical hatch system, the diameter of which is less than 30in. This means all stores and supplies must be handed up and down by chains of sailors. In this way the modern fast attack submarine is little different from the 18th-century sailing warship.

budget cycle came around, the Tang design was six years old, and a new design was needed to keep pace with the Soviets.

The Navy, using the salvaged engine room from *U-1406* and a 7,500hp turbine from a German Type XXVI, tested the closed-cycle Walter system at Annapolis in 1945–47. The Walter design was the type used in the Type XXVI, and used hydrogen peroxide as an oxidant to be combined with a fuel to drive either an engine or turbine. One of the initial Tang designs envisaged using two of the turbines with the Walter system; however, this system was so large it wouldn't fit in the proposed hull. Other alternative submarine propulsion designs were studied. These included two gas turbine semi-enclosed systems, an external combustion condensing cycle, the free-piston gas generator or gas turbine cycle, the closed-cycle diesel system, and the nuclear reactor steam propulsion system. As testing on the alternatives to diesel-electric propulsion progressed, the size of the submarine required to carry the systems grew. By 1952, therefore, the nuclear option had grown so attractive that it was adopted.

Going nuclear

The possibility of nuclear propulsion in naval vessels had been under consideration since 1939 and under active engineering planning since 1947. Studies were undertaken to determine the best design for the propulsion plant and in August 1949 it became clear that a nuclear-powered submarine could be and should be built. The nuclear propulsion plant married a new technology with an old one. The old one was the steam turbine marine propulsion plant. This was tested, battle tested, and refined to be an efficient and lightweight (in terms of weight-to-horsepower ratio) shipboard system. The new technology was the means of generating the steam. A nuclear reactor is a means of using a controlled nuclear fission reaction to produce a desired quantity of heat energy, which in a submarine could be transferred to a boiler to generate the steam that drove the turbines. Using a nuclear reactor as a primary energy source for propulsion and electrical generation had big advantages in that the propulsion plant would not require outside air to operate, nor would it require the storage of volatile oxidants such as hydrogen peroxide.

Various experiments and engineering studies were underway to determine how best to use this heat source for power production. These centered around two areas. First was the type of nuclear fission to be used and the second was how to transfer the heat energy from the reactor core so it could be useful. Types of nuclear fission included thermal fission using enriched Uranium and fast fission with enriched Uranium, and the use of other fissile materials such as Plutonium was also considered. Heat energy transfer methods included pressurized

PLATE A
The transition from the diesel-electric "fleet type" submarine to the production "nuclear fast attack" not only changed the size of submarines but produced a fundamental change in their shape. The fleet type design (1) had to compromise a good submerged performance hull form with the need to be seaworthy on the surface where it spent most of its time. The Tang Class diesel-electric fast attack design (2) smoothed much of the hull form to decrease drag. From the Nautilus design (3) was learned a great deal about high-speed submerged ship characteristics. It still retained a small superstructure for surfaced operations. The Skate Class design (4) was the first "production design" nuclear fast attack.

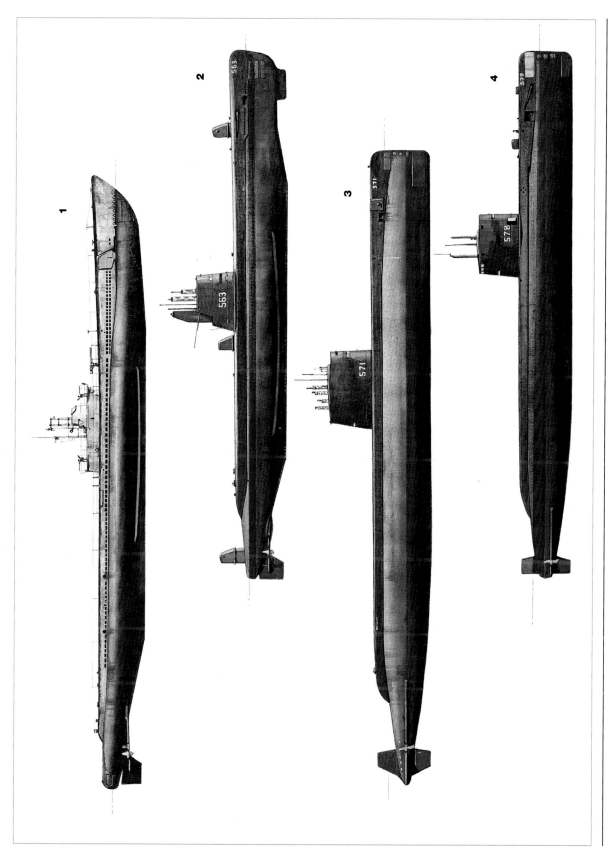

1

2

3

4

water, pressurized gases, and liquid-metal mediums. In the end, the pressurized water thermal reactor proved to be the most attractive. The use and refinement of this system produced what has become the standard nuclear propulsion plant for surface ships and submarines.

The SCB called for a specific design, SCB 64, to be part of the FY52 building program. The ship was to prove revolutionary in more than its propulsion. Its design required advances in areas that were not necessary on previous submarines. The steam plant produced a great quantity of heat that had to be controlled by increasing the size of air-conditioning systems. The ability of the boat to stay underwater for long periods of time meant that the air had to be cleansed of carbon dioxide and the oxygen replenished. Sonar performance characteristics changed because the submarine would not be making attacks while surfaced. Navigation systems had to be rethought and made independent of the standard methods that used the sun and stars for locating.

In January 1954 the world's first nuclear-powered vessel, the USS *Nautilus* (SSN-571), sent a radio message "Underway on nuclear power." The *Nautilus* proved that high underwater speed and long endurance were possible, and the US Navy needed to ensure it was ready for threats with the same capability. Antisubmarine warfare (ASW) tactics and strategies had to be rethought all over the world. Submarines could now travel huge distances completely out of sight and could operate unseen in any ocean. Not only did *Nautilus* change the future of submarines, but it also altered the future course of all naval warfare.

Nautilus Class

The USS *Nautilus* was a big submarine. It had three decks and plenty of internal space compared with the fleet submarine. Alongside its ability to stay completely submerged nearly indefinitely, it was fast. A Tench Class fleet submarine could run at 22 knots on the surface and a Tang Class diesel-electric could make 18 knots in a short burst or 11 knots snorkeling. *Nautilus* could make 23 knots while remaining completely submerged for months. It could evade destroyer screens, run in and attack escorted

USS *Nautilus* makes its triumphant entry into New York Harbor after crossing from the Pacific to the Atlantic under the Arctic ice. She demonstrated in stunning fashion that the Arctic Ocean could be traversed, and opened it for submarine operations that continue to this day.

high-value targets, and run out again. The down-side of this speed was a very high noise level. Its ballast tank flood ports and its relatively thin plating made a humming sound that varied in frequency and intensity with speed. It has been said that the noise was so loud it prevented any conversation in the torpedo room except by shouting. *Nautilus* had a BQR-4 passive sonar system. The 48 vertical stave hydrophones wrapped around just inside the skin of a sonar dome that was faired into the forefoot of the boat. This sonar system was useless at any appreciable speed because of the noise created by the ship itself. However, using sprint and wait tactics, *Nautilus* proved to be a dangerous adversary. During one of her first tactical trials she demonstrated a greater threat than all the accompanying diesel-electric submarines combined.

Nautilus had six torpedo tubes forward in the torpedo room. The crew and officers' berthing and messing spaces were located aft of the torpedo room. The control room and conning stations were farther aft under her large sail (or "fin" in Royal Navy nomenclature). Just over half the ship was taken up by the reactor compartment and engine room. The reactor compartment housed the reactor, primary coolant piping, steam generators, and attendant systems. It was not a manned space and was only accessible if the reactor was shut down. Passage fore and aft took place through a narrow shielded space at the top of the reactor compartment, which came to be called "the tunnel."

With the steam plant came a few benefits not generally available to diesel-electric boat sailors. The first was a large quantity of fresh water for cooking and personal use. Water for showers and bathing was very limited, if available at all, on diesel-electric subs. The second benefit was air conditioning. Having a steam plant in an enclosed space demanded some method of dealing with heat build-up, but a large amount of available electricity allowed for major air-conditioning plants to be installed and operated. These increased the level of habitability to a point not seen on previous boats.

Nautilus' stern. The propulsion shafts were faired into a fixed portion of the stern plane structure. The moveable part is seen here angled down. The fairing around the rudder and planes was not repeated. Along the side above the planes are a set of small tabbed rectangles. These are sacrificial anidodes that help control dissimilar metal corrosion.

NAUTILUS CLASS

Design designator EB251A, SCB-64
Class consists of one ship: USS *Nautilus* (SSN-571)
Dimensions Length 323ft 9in.; beam 27ft 9in.
Displacement (surfaced/submerged) 3,533/4,092 tons
Speed (surfaced/submerged) 23/23.3 knots
Endurance Only limited by supplies
Design test depth See author's note
Complement (officer/enlisted) 13/92
Armament Torpedo tubes: six Mk 50 torpedo tubes (23ft long by 21in. diameter).
   The tubes and fire-control systems are capable of handling various types
   of torpedo (Mk 14-6, Mk 16-6, -8, Mk 37-1, -3).
Service history:
   Laid down 14-Jun-52
   Launched 21-Jan-54
   Commissioned 30-Sep-54
   Decommissioned 30-Mar-80
   Final disposition Designated as Historic Ship *Nautilus*, and is the centerpiece
      of the Submarine Force Library and Museum in Groton, CT

Skate Class

A second nuclear-powered submarine was already being built when *Nautilus* took to the water. The USS *Seawolf* (SSN-575) was smaller and initially had a reactor system that used liquid sodium as a moderator and heat-transfer medium rather than water. This system, although attractive because it reduced the size of the primary plant, was deemed too difficult to maintain and was discarded after ship testing. The reactor plant was replaced with a pressurized water plant.

A production model of a nuclear submarine was on the drawing board at the time. This, a Skate Class, would be smaller than *Nautilus* and *Seawolf* but incorporated some of the lessons learned from initial operations of *Nautilus*. These three classes (Nautilus, Seawolf, Skate) held on to many of the design features of the diesel-electric fleet submarines. The hull shape was similar to the Tang Class to keep some form of surfaced seakeeping. The propulsion system had twin screws to provide redundant power – if one screw or one side of the engine room were to become damaged, the ship could still maneuver and travel with the other screw.

Much smaller and somewhat more crowded than *Nautilus*, the Skates proved to be exceptionally useful. The reactor compartment and engine rooms were smaller and more compact. The boats were slower than *Nautilus* but their submerged endurance still allowed them freedom of operation that diesel-electrics could not match. The operations compartment and torpedo rooms were rearranged to provide more efficiency in conning and combat management. Following the lead of *Nautilus*, USS *Skate* transited submerged in the Arctic, but, going one better, she surfaced at the North Pole. USS *Seadragon* (SSN-584) completed the transit in a reverse manner, from the Atlantic to the Pacific.

SKATE CLASS

Design designator EB264A

Class consists of four ships: USS *Skate*, USS *Sargo*, USS *Swordfish*, and USS *Seadragon*

Dimensions Length 267ft 8in.; beam 25ft

Displacement (surfaced/submerged) 2,550/2,848 tons

Speed (surfaced/submerged) See author's note

Endurance Only limited by supplies

Design test depth See author's note

Complement (officer/enlisted) 8/76

Armament Torpedo tubes: six Mk 56 forward (23ft long by 21in. diameter); two Mk 57 aft (18ft long by 21in. diameter). The tubes and fire-control systems are capable of handling various types of torpedo (Mk 14-6, Mk 16-6, -8, Mk 37-1, -3), the longer torpedoes from the forward tubes only.

Service history:

	Laid down	Launched	Commissioned	Decommissioned
USS *Skate* (SSN-578)	21-Jul-55	16-May-57	23-Dec-57	12-Sep-86
USS *Swordfish* (SSN-579)	25-Jan-56	27-Aug-57	15-Sep-58	2-Jun-89
USS *Sargo* (SSN-583)	21-Feb-56	10-Oct-57	1-Oct-58	26-Feb-88
USS *Seadragon* (SSN-584)	20-Jun-56	16-Aug-58	5-Dec-59	12-Jun-84

All these ships have been disposed of by the SRP.

Skipjack Class

As the design cycle for the Skate Class was coming to a close and all the boats of the class were either built or being built, the Navy was looking at making another profound change in submarine design. Back in 1900 John Phillip Holland in his Design #6, which was to become the USS *Holland* (SS-1), created a hull form for underwater travel. It had a screw aft of the rudder, stern planes, and a minimal superstructure. During its sea trials, Holland found that a submarine with a single screw and the rudder forward of the screw was nearly unmanageable at slow speed

The USS *Skate* became the first vessel in history to surface at the North Pole. During her visit, in March 1959, the crew held a memorial service and scattered the ashes of the famed explorer Sir Hubert Wilkins, who had died the previous November. Sir Hubert had refitted an O Class US submarine to explore under the Arctic ice in 1931. His expedition reached the ice pack and briefly dove under, proving it was indeed possible. The submarine he used, which he had renamed the *Nautilus*, was scuttled in a fjord near Bergen, Norway, where it remains to this day.

The USS *Holland*, first of the commissioned submarines in the US Navy, shows the hull form adopted nearly 60 years later for efficient underwater performance.

(slow was his only real choice of speed). This lesson was relearned by the Navy 60 years later. However, the hull form was adopted and studied in the experimental submarine *Albacore* and the three diesel-electric submarines *Barbel*, *Bonefish*, and *Blueback*.

The shift to a single screw was not popular with everyone but it was shown that to maximize the underwater speed of a submarine with a given shp, a "cylinder of revolution" teardrop hull form with a relatively low length-to-beam ratio was desirable. The new class of submarine, which matched an upgraded and somewhat larger nuclear powerplant with the new hull form, was the Skipjack Class. Here was a submarine that approached what we know of today as nuclear fast attack capability. The short, "fat" hull shape combined with a smooth outer surface, made the boat very fast indeed, with a speed of over 25 knots (it was even faster than the design group had hoped.) Skipjack also had a smaller superstructure than the Skate, thus had less hydrodynamic resistance even though it had a larger volume. It was shorter than *Nautilus* but had a more efficient use of internal volume.

The sail on the Skipjack Class was enormous. This gave it good seakeeping ability at periscope depth because of the vertical separation between the top of the sail (from which her masts, periscopes, and antenna protruded) and the top of the pressure hull. The forward hydroplanes were moved from their normal position near the bow, cutting down on the amount of flow noise affecting the bow-mounted sonar arrays. The shape and smoothness of the hull made the sonar, still the venerable BQR-4B, more effective at a higher speed, but the machinery noise remained a serious problem. The sail had a small "turtleback" that ran from the lower trailing edge nearly to the engine-room hatch. This housed the emergency diesel exhaust piping, which couldn't be run through the reactor compartment. The large sail, this turtleback, and the short fat hull made the Skipjacks very identifiable.

The Skipjack Class was a long-lived one and was very comfortable for the crew. A relatively large torpedo room allowed for additional crew berthing, and the crew and officer messing spaces were comfortably large.

Mr Morton Gertler, a naval architect, is shown with Mr Carson W. Caudle with a model of the USS *Albacore*. This model was tested at the David Taylor Ship Test Facility and showed that the streamlined hull was the shape of the future. Note the similarities between this and the USS *Holland*, designed and built 50 years earlier.

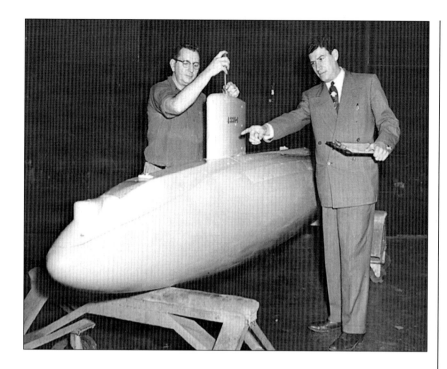

The engineering spaces were divided into the engine room and a large auxiliary machinery space between the engine room and reactor compartment. Much of the electrical distribution switchgear and switchboards, along with the electronics for reactor control and instrumentation, was situated in the auxiliary machinery space. This arrangement moved the electrical and electronic equipment away from the steamplant spaces proper to allow a more controlled (dry and oil-free) atmosphere, thus enhancing reliability.

SKIPJACK CLASS

Design designator EB269A

Class consisted of six ships: USS *Skipjack*, USS *Scamp*, USS *Scorpion*, USS *Sculpin*, USS *Shark*, and USS *Snook*

Dimensions Length 251ft 9in.; beam 31ft 9in.

Displacement (surfaced/submerged) 3,070/3,500 tons

Speed (surfaced/submerged) See author's note

Endurance Only limited by supplies

Design test depth See author's note

Complement (officer/enlisted) 9/76

Armament Torpedo tubes: six Mk 59 (23ft long by 21in. diameter). The tubes and fire-control systems were capable of handling various types of torpedo (Mk 14-6, Mk 16-6, -8, Mk 37-1, -3).

Service history:

	Laid down	Launched	Commissioned	Decommissioned
USS *Skipjack* (SSN-585)	29-May-56	26-May-58	15-Apr-59	19-Apr-90
USS *Scamp* (SSN-588)	23-Jan-59	8-Oct-60	5-Jun-61	28-Apr-88
USS *Scorpion* (SSN-589)	20-Aug-58	19-Dec-59	29-Jul-60	LOST 21-May-68
USS *Sculpin* (SSN-590)	3-Feb-58	31-Mar-60	1-Jun-61	3-Aug-90
USS *Shark* (SSN-591)	24-Feb-58	16-Mar-60	9-Feb-61	15-Sep-90
USS *Snook* (SSN-592)	7-Apr-58	31-Oct-60	24-Oct-61	16-Oct-86

All these ships have been disposed of by the SRP.

A Barbel Class submarine in dry dock. The feasibility of the hull shape for modern submarine use was proven by the experimental submarine the USS *Albacore* and became the standard for all modern nuclear submarines. Note also the forward hydroplanes which were moved from the bow to the sail in this class.

Thresher and Permit classes

Halfway through the Skipjack Class design cycle, about 1957, a new submarine design went to the drawing board. It was to become the Thresher Class. This was the first of the true fast attack submarines. It had an improved sonar concept with a 16ft spherical array in the bow. The torpedo tubes were moved aft and slanted outward. The hull form as designed was going to be slower than Skipjack because it used the same powerplant on a larger hull, so other changes were made to increase speed. The sail was made smaller and thinner with the sacrifice of some periscope depth controlability and the type and number of sensor masts.

One of the main reasons for the enlarged hull was noise quieting. To complement the increased sonar capabilities, the new class had to be fast and quiet. Submarine quieting is an engineering problem that is simple in concept and extremely difficult in execution. Conceptually, sound consists of three elements: a noise source, a receiver, and a transmission path between the source and the receiver. In the case of submarine silencing, the receiver is the enemy's sonar. The transmission path consists

PLATE B
A fundamental change in submarine shape took place, as shown here, when the hull form took on what is known as a "body of revolution," meaning that each hull section was a circle and the center of each circle was on the same centerline. The Barbel Class (**1**) was an attempt to produce a diesel-electric fast attack with good underwater performance. It still suffered from a lack of range when completely submerged. The Skipjack Class (**2**) was far and away the fastest submarine in the world until the Los Angeles Class. Below the Skipjack is the Thresher/Permit Class (**3**) which had the same power plant as Skipjack but in a slightly larger hull. Although somewhat slower than Skipjack, it was quieter and is called by many the first true nuclear fast attack class. At the bottom is the Sturgeon Class (**4**). Bigger than the Thresher/Permit it had a robustness and versatility that set the standard for performance and usefulness.

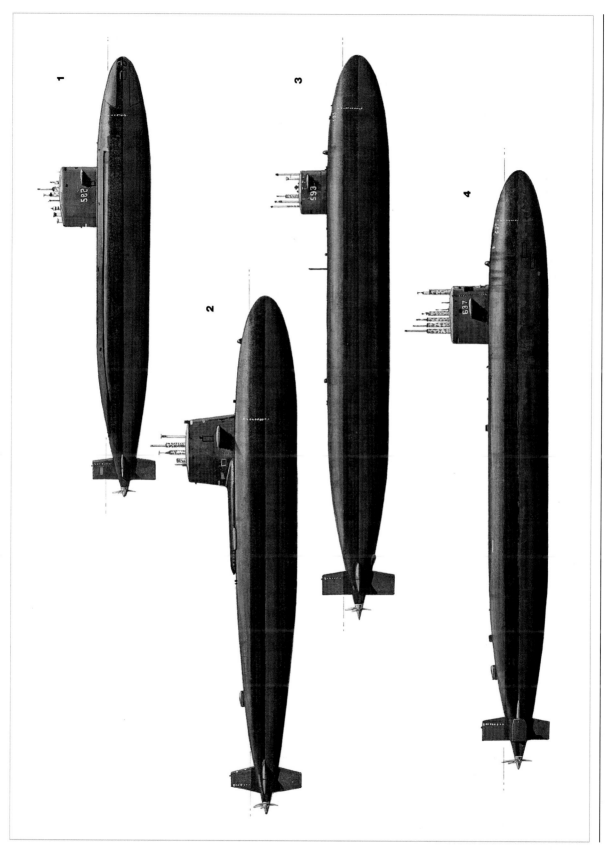

of everything between the noise generation source and the sonar – this includes the equipment foundation, any intermediate structure, the hull, and the external water column. The amount of noise that reaches the enemy sonar depends on the amount of noise the source generates, the directness and efficiency of the structure-borne noise paths, and the transmissibility of the water column. As the enemy's sonar becomes more effective (able to detect and analyze a lower level noise signal), it is able to detect a given noise source level at greater distances. To defeat this detection ability, the submarine must lower the noise source level and/or interrupt the structure-borne transmission path.

Most of the noise a submarine generates comes from rotating machinery within the hull – pumps, motors, fans, and so on. To make them quieter is feasible but expensive. Equipment must be maintained with great care. Each noise producer must be designed to be as quiet as possible. Now comes the hard part. Each noise producer must be separated from the hull by noise isolation devices commonly called sound mounts. Attention to detail is the key here. Not only must the small equipment be sound mounted, reducing noises such as flow noise in piping, transformer hum, and so on, but also the largest items such as the main propulsion turbines and turbine generators. Naval architects used the British rafting design for major equipment in the engine room. To complicate matters still further any single hard, non-isolated connection between a noise source and the hull could defeat the entire program. Such a connection is called a sound short. It takes a great deal of design work and care in construction to create a noise-quieted submarine and even more detailed maintenance and operational care by the crew and any overhaul shipyards to keep the boat quiet. In addition, it means the submarine needs to be a bit bigger than one in which there is no silencing.

The first ship of the Thresher Class was the USS *Thresher*. It was commissioned in August 1961 and spent much of its early life in "first of class" testing. On April 10, 1963, while undergoing routine testing after a period of routine shipyard work, she was lost with all hands and a large

Skipjack Class from the bow. Note the distance from the sail planes to the top of the sail and compare this with the photo of Thresher. The Skipjack Class was much easier to handle at periscope depth than the Thresher Class.

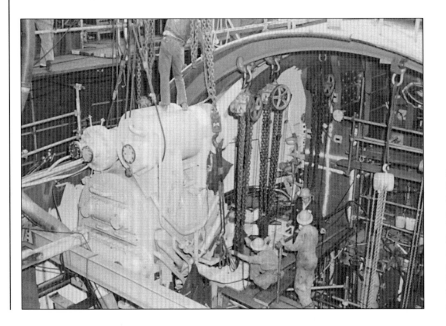

An air-conditioning unit is lowered into the hull of the boat during the construction of a Permit Class submarine. The use of a steam plant in a closed submarine hull demanded the use of significant air conditioning to deal with the heat. Note the internal hull frames in this single hull portion of the submarine.

contingent of shipyard engineers and test technicians. The loss sent ripples throughout the submarine community and not only for its loss – if there was a design flaw, it was being duplicated in the other Thresher Class boats being built and planned. The boat lay in 8,300ft of water off the coast of Maine and was not available for detailed inspection. What followed was a serious look at how the submarine force ensured quality of maintenance and material, and the result was the SubSafe Program. Everything that touches or is connected to the hull and every system or device is rigorously quality-controlled and/or pressure tested through the SubSafe Program.

The class name was changed after *Thresher*'s loss – it became the Permit Class. Even though the class was longer than the Skipjacks, it seemed to be – at least to the author, who was stationed aboard both Skipjack Class (USS *Scamp*) and Permit Class (USS *Dace*) vessels – to be more crowded and less efficiently laid out. There were increased amounts of equipment aboard and increased space taken up by noise quieting efforts. The torpedo room was rearranged and moved aft and to the lower level of the operations compartment. This move was motivated by the placement of the new sonar system, which had as its central sensor a passive array on a 16ft steel sphere mounted just outside the pressure hull in the bow. The large array could "listen" up and down through a wide arc and side to side through nearly 270 degrees. Its inboard electronics were an analog system designated as the BQR-6A and integrated with a set of Passive Underwater Firecontrol Feasibility Study (PUFFS) collinearly aligned planar arrays (BQG-4). The collection of sonar sensors was generally called the BQQ-1. The complexity of the system and that of its hydrophone selection and switching system led to a high failure rate and increased maintenance over older, less-complicated systems. As the class became older, the BQQ-5 was backfitted onto many of the boats, increasing their sonar capability.

The lower, thinner sail on the Permit Class gave reduced drag, but was operationally more limited because of less space for periscopes and masts. Its height also meant more difficult seakeeping at periscope depth. The periscope was sited aft of the snorkel mast, a location that limited visibility while the submarine was ventilating and snorkeling. The emergency diesel generator was moved forward and hence eliminated the distinctive turtleback seen on Skipjacks.

As the SubSafe Program took hold, the space required to implement the elements of the program increased. Some portions of the system required new equipment and piping. For example, air dryers were required on the high-pressure side of the air compressors to ensure the 3,000psi air system, which was used for, amongst other things, blowing ballast tanks, was free from moisture which could form ice in valves and pressure reducers. One of the possible problems encountered by *Thresher*, proven later by testing similarly designed systems, was that

THRESHER/PERMIT CLASS

Design designator SCB 166A

Class consists of 15 ships starting with USS *Thresher* and ending with USS *Haddock*

Dimensions Length 278ft 6in. (see remarks); beam 31ft 9in.

Displacement (surfaced/submerged) 3,070/3,500 tons

Speed (surfaced/submerged) See author's note

Endurance Only limited by supplies

Design test depth See author's note

Complement (officer/enlisted) 9/76

Armament Torpedo tubes: four Mk 63 (23ft long by 21in. diameter). The tubes and fire-control systems are capable of handling various types of torpedo: Mk 16, Mk 37 Mod 3, Mk 48, Mk 48 ADCAP. In addition they carried the SubRoc (Submarine Rocket) and in later years the Harpoon antiship missile.

Remarks Ship class designation was changed to Permit Class after the loss of USS *Thresher* on April 10, 1963. There were various lengths and sail heights within this class. SSN-593, 594, 595, 596, 603, 604, 606, 607, 612, and 621 were 278ft 6in. long, SSN-605 was 297ft 4in. long, and SSN-613, 614, and 615 were 292ft 3in. long. USS *Jack* was significantly different, having a different main propulsion turbine arrangement with counter-rotating screws, but it is included in this class.

Service history:

	Laid down	Launched	Commissioned	Decommissioned
USS *Thresher* (SSN-593)	28-May-58	9-Jul-60	3-Aug-61	LOST 10-Apr-63
USS *Permit* (SSN-594)	16-Jul-59	1-Jul-61	29-May-62	23-Jul-91
USS *Plunger* (SSN-595)	2-Mar-60	9-Dec-61	21-Nov-62	3-Jan-90
USS *Barb* (SSN-596)	9-Nov-59	12-Feb-62	24-Aug-63	20-Dec-89
USS *Tullibee* (SSN-597)	26-May-58	27-Apr-60	9-Nov-60	25-Jun-88
USS *Pollack* (SSN-603)	14-Mar-60	17-Mar-62	26-May-64	1-Mar-89
USS *Haddo* (SSN-604)	9-Sep-60	18-Aug-62	16-Dec-64	12-Jun-91
USS *Jack* (SSN-605)	16-Sep-60	24-Apr-63	31-Mar-67	11-Jul-90
USS *Tinosa* (SSN-606)	24-Nov-59	9-Dec-61	17-Oct-64	15-Jan-92
USS *Dace* (SSN-607)	6-Jun-60	18-Aug-62	4-Apr-64	2-Dec-88
USS *Guardfish* (SSN-612)	13-Feb-61	15-May-65	20-Dec-66	4-Feb-92
USS *Flasher* (SSN-613)	14-Apr-61	22-Jun-63	22-Jul-66	14-Sep-92
USS *Greenling* (SSN-614)	15-Aug-61	4-Apr-64	3-Nov-67	18-Apr-94
USS *Gato* (SSN-615)	15-Dec-61	14-May-64	25-Jan-68	25-Apr-96
USS *Haddock* (SSN-621)	24-Apr-61	21-May-66	22-Dec-67	7-Apr-93

All these ships have been disposed of by the SRP.

moisture in the air tended to freeze in ballast blow hull valves. This would not be a problem unless the boat needed to blow a second time soon after the initial blow, as *Thresher* had to do. In addition, the entire high-pressure emergency ballast tank blow system had to be redesigned, and the reengineering required the use of a new, larger piping system and electrically operated blow valves. Engineering-space hydraulics and valve placement had to be redesigned to antennae with the requirement that all hull valves could be closed from a central location (the maneuvering room) and a very few local positions. Some of the Permits were lengthened, but the new requirements and new equipment actually required a new submarine design.

Sturgeon Class

The new design, which became the Sturgeon Class, had a hull that was 292ft long, a gain of just over 13ft, and the sail size was significantly increased. The Permits, due to their increased length over the Skipjacks, were nearly 3 knots slower. The Sturgeon Class was longer still and had the same power plant, so was in turn nearly 3 knots slower than the Permits. However, it had SubSafe from the start and was also much quieter. The design benefited from lessons learnt from the late Permits about equipment arrangements, and Sturgeon Class vessels were viewed by their crews to be comfortable boats. In fact, more than one crewman remembered an unofficial motto of the class as being "Give me heaven or a 637." They were considered by most who sailed them to be the ultimate fast attack submarines. They were capable, versatile, and comfortable and they made hard, long deployments. It was not unknown for some to spend 300 days out of home port in a year. Underway times between port calls could be as long as 90 days and these boats could load stores and be back underway in as little as 24 hours.

The consoles of the control center for controlling the movement of a Sturgeon Class boat underwater. The two seats are for the helm, bow (or fairwater) planes, and stern plane operators. The far console is the Ballast Control Panel (BCP). The operator there controlled the trim of the submarine and pumped water in and out to control the buoyancy. This picture is of the Ship Control Center which was on display at the Smithsonian Institution Museum of American History in Washington, DC. (Smithsonian Institution: National Museum of American History)

STURGEON CLASS

Design designator EB293A

Class consists of 38 ships from USS *Sturgeon* to USS *Richard B. Russell*. However, the hull numbers are not sequential due to the SSBN-640 Class and two "one-off" exceptions. Therefore included in the class are SSN-637, 638, 639, 646 through 653, 660 through 670, 672 through 684, 686 and 687.

Dimensions Length 292ft; beam 31ft 9in.

Displacement (surfaced/submerged) 4,229/4,762 tons

Speed (surfaced/submerged) See author's note

Endurance Only limited by supplies

Design test depth See author's note

Complement (officer/enlisted) 12/95

Armament: Torpedo tubes: four Mk 67 (23ft long by 21in. diameter), angled outward from midships. Bow contained sonar spherical array. The tubes and fire-control systems were capable of handling various types of torpedo (Mk 37-3, Mk 37 NTS, Mk 48, Mk 48 ADCAP), SubRoc, Harpoon, and Tomahawk missiles.

Service history:

	Laid down	Launched	Commissioned	Decommissioned
USS *Sturgeon* (SSN-637)	10-Aug-63	26-Feb-66	3-Mar-67	1-Aug-94
USS *Whale* (SSN-638)	27-May-64	14-Oct-66	12-Oct-68	25-Jun-96
USS *Tautog* (SSN-639)	27-Jan-64	15-Apr-67	17-Aug-68	31-Mar-97
USS *Grayling* (SSN-646)	12-May-64	22-Jun-67	11-Oct-69	18-Jul-97
USS *Pogy* (SSN-647)	4-May-64	3-Jun-67	15-May-71	11-Jun-99
USS *Aspro* (SSN-648)	23-Nov-64	29-Nov-67	20-Feb-69	31-Mar-95
USS *Sunfish* (SSN-649)	15-Jan-65	14-Oct-66	15-Mar-69	31-Mar-97
USS *Pargo* (SSN-650)	3-Jun-64	17-Sep-66	5-Jan-68	14-Apr-95
USS *Queenfish* (SSN-651)	11-May-64	25-Feb-66	6-Dec-66	14-Apr-92
USS *Puffer* (SSN-652)	8-Feb-65	30-Mar-68	9-Aug-69	12-Jul-96
USS *Ray* (SSN-653)	4-Jan-65	21-Jun-66	12-Apr-67	16-Mar-93
USS *Sand Lance* (SSN-660)	15-Jan-65	11-Nov-69	25-Sep-71	7-Aug-98
USS *Lapon* (SSN-661)	26-Jul-65	16-Dec-66	14-Dec-67	8-Aug-92
USS *Gurnard* (SSN-662)	22-Dec-64	20-May-67	6-Dec-68	28-Apr-95
USS *Hammerhead* (SSN-663)	29-Nov-65	14-Apr-67	28-Jun-68	5-Apr-95
USS *Sea Devil* (SSN-664)	12-Apr-65	5-Oct-67	30-Jan-69	16-Oct-91
USS *Guitarro* (SSN-665)	9-Dec-65	27-Jul-68	9-Sep-72	29-May-92
USS *Hawkbill* (SSN-666)	12-Sep-66	12-Apr-69	4-Feb-71	15-Mar-00
USS *Bergall* (SSN-667)	16-Apr-66	17-Feb-68	13-Jun-69	6-Jun-97
USS *Spadefish* (SSN-668)	21-Dec-66	15-May-68	14-Aug-69	11-Apr-97
USS *Seahorse* (SSN-669)	13-Aug-66	15-Jun-68	19-Sep-69	17-Aug-95
USS *Finback* (SSN-670)	26-Jun-67	7-Dec-68	4-Feb-70	28-Mar-97
USS *Narwhal* (SSN-671)	17-Jan-66	9-Sep-67	12-Jul-69	1-Jul-99
USS *Pintado* (SSN-672)	27-Oct-67	16-Aug-69	11-Sep-71	26-Feb-98
USS *Flying Fish* (SSN-673)	30-Jun-67	17-May-69	29-Apr-70	16-May-96
USS *Trepang* (SSN-674)	28-Oct-67	27-Sep-69	14-Aug-70	1-Jun-99
USS *Bluefish* (SSN-675)	13-Mar-68	10-Jan-70	8-Jan-71	31-May-96
USS *Billfish* (SSN-676)	20-Sep-68	1-May-70	12-Mar-71	1-Jul-99
USS *Drum* (SSN-677)	20-Aug-68	23-May-70	15-Apr-72	30-Oct-95
USS *Archerfish* (SSN-678)	19-Jun-69	16-Jan-71	17-Dec-71	31-Mar-98
USS *Silversides* (SSN-679)	28-Nov-69	4-Jun-71	5-May-72	21-Jul-94
USS *William H. Bates* (SSN-680)	4-Aug-69	11-Dec-71	5-May-73	11-Feb-00
USS *Batfish* (SSN-681)	9-Feb-70	9-Oct-71	1-Sep-72	17-Mar-99
USS *Tunny* (SSN-682)	22-May-70	10-Jun-72	26-Jan-74	13-Mar-98
USS *Parche* (SSN-683)	10-Dec-70	13-Jan-73	17-Aug-74	18-Jul-05
USS *Cavalla* (SSN-684)	23-May-70	19-Feb-72	9-Feb-73	30-Mar-98
USS *L. Mendel Rivers* (SSN-686)	26-Jun-71	2-Jun-73	1-Feb-75	10-May-01
USS *Richard B. Russell* (SSN-687)	19-Oct-71	12-Jan-74	16-Aug-75	24-Jun-94

All these ships have been disposed of by the SRP.

The Sturgeons were able to rotate their fairwater planes 90 degrees and had a hardened sail top. This made it possible to break through a significant thickness of ice. The dark portion of the sail front is the sound-transparent cover over the upward-looking sonar receiver.

Los Angeles Class

In the late 1960s it was obvious to naval planners that the Soviets were in the midst of a submarine construction program of their own, one that included a serious requirement for high speed. The trend in US submarines, however, seemed to be toward slower boats. The Soviet Union was building fast boats that would dive deeper than the existing US vessels, hence a new design was needed that would fulfill three main objectives: dive deep, be fast, and be quiet at high speed. The design process, however, was to be difficult.

Naval Sea Systems Command (NavSea), which replaced BuShips, started the design cycle in 1966 for a fast submarine to replace the Sturgeon and Permit classes as they reached the end of their useful lives. This new submarine would have to be proficient in five mission types. They were:

Forward area – operations in the waters close to enemy bases.
Trailing – operations in which the boat had to acquire contact with an enemy vessel and follow it undetected. Enemy vessels were to include, but were not limited to, enemy ballistic missile submarines.
Direct support of battle groups – operations as part of a defensive screen.
Attacks on enemy submarines and surface ships.
Surveillance – special operations (SEAL team deployment), training etc.

The new design would not simply be an upgrade from the existing Sturgeon, it would be a whole new submarine with a new, more capable powerplant.

US Naval nuclear powerplants are designated by a letter/number combination. First is a letter S, D, or A. The letter S means a submarine plant, D is for surface craft such as destroyers and cruisers, and A is for aircraft carriers. The number starts with 1 and proceeds upward with newer plants, and the final letter, C, W, or G is for the manufacturer – Combustion Engineering, Westinghouse, and General Electric respectively. The Skipjacks, Permits, and Sturgeons used an excellent design that

The USS *Columbia* was the penultimate Los Angeles Class submarine to be built and the last "slider" – that is, she slid down the inclined building ways into the water like countless ships before her. All US submarines built after her are built in level building facilities and floated into a graving dock for launch.

became a true workhorse, the S5W plant. NavSea wanted to marry a submarine version of the more powerful D1G with a new front end. Another option would be an up-powered S5G natural circulation plant that was being proven on USS *Narwhal.*

The Navy had to follow a new set of rules about selecting ship design. Robert McNamara was the new Secretary of Defense and his business background at Ford led him to institute a complex design process called CONFORM (Concept Formulation). This system called for a detailed study of all possible combinations of existing and future technologies and needs. Such design studies took time and cost money. Also, the CONFORM studies were in addition to the standard engineering work that had to be done just to write the specifications for the new submarine design. The CONFORM process came at a time when it seemed imperative that the United States produce a fast submarine design and build them quickly, so the two requirements were in conflict.

The actual work started with a pre-design trade-off study and the CONFORM study began in late 1968. Trade-off studies assess the best balance of engine power/ship size/armament for the most efficiently balanced design. A completely new all-digital sonar and fire-control system was specified in 1966 and would have to be included. A new propulsion plant would have to go through the CONFORM process – it could not simply be chosen by the Nuclear Propulsion Directorate – and the process had to be completed in its entirety before a new submarine design specification could be written. The new submarine design became bogged down in administration, but McNamara subsequently left and the new Secretary of Defense, Clark Clifford, scrapped the CONFORM system altogether. Fresh design specifications rapidly emerged. The new boats would be 360ft long with a beam of 33ft. The reactor plant, newly designated S6G, had sufficient shp to give a design speed in excess of 30 knots, which was faster than the Skipjacks. These boats, which were nearly as large as World War II

An early Los Angeles Class. The darker portion in the foreground is the fiberglass sonar dome. The lighter part is the smooth hull reflecting ambient light and the darker upper deck has grit-laden non-skid paint. The light circular object is the mooring line properly flemished down. The two masts raised highest are the BRA-34 multipurpose antennae.

The stern cone of a fast attack submarine is prepared to be lifted off the transporter. Protruding to the right is the fixed portion of the stern planes. At the left is the opening for the stern tube through which the propeller shaft will extend.

light cruisers, would be named after US cities under the umbrella of the Los Angeles Class.

The Los Angeles Class is quieter at speed than any other submarine to date, and the S6G powerplant has fulfilled the design speed of more than 30 knots. The sonar sphere is placed well forward and the dome wrapped around it is of sound-transparent fiberglass. The sonar's inboard electronics are all digital with the Mk 117 fire-control system. As the first of the class were nearing completion and reaching the fleet, the integration of the sensors and fire-control systems reached a point where they could be incorporated into several common consoles linked by a local network, and whose function was dictated by the common UYK-7 computer software and hardware. This system was called the BSY-1. Later versions of this concept were called the Combat Control System (CCS) Mk 1 and 2. Although the Tomahawk cruise missile was torpedo-tube capable, it was decided to make a major modification to the class design and mount 12 vertical launch tubes in the bows of the remainder of the class, starting with SSN-719. In addition, the fairwater planes were relocated to the bow – the planes in the sail were too large to rotate 90 degrees to allow for under-ice operations. For grouping purposes, there are three main variants of the Los Angeles Class. The first group are the *Los Angeles* (SSN-688) to *Honolulu* (SSN-618) which are the original design with only minor variations. *Providence* (SSN-619) through *Newport News* (SSN-750) have sail planes and vertical launch tubes (note that hull numbers 726 through 749 were reserved for the Ohio Class ballistic missile submarines) and comprise the second grouping. The *San Juan* (SSN-751) through the end of the class *Cheyenne* (SSN-773), which are called the Los Angeles Improved or 688I, had bow planes and vertical launch tubes.

C: INTERIOR LAYOUT OF A LOS ANGELES CLASS SUBMARINE

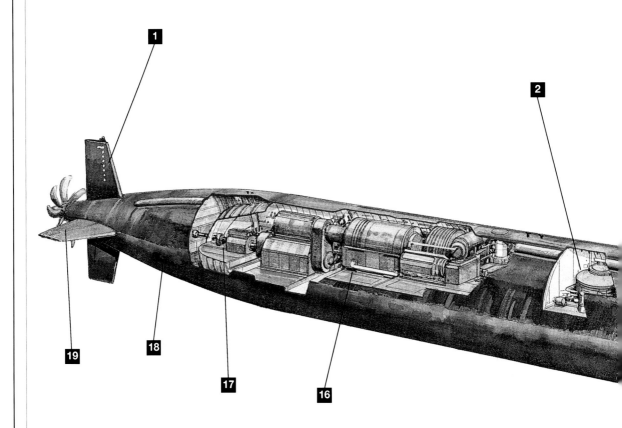

The Los Angeles Class is divided into three general areas. First are the fore and aft ballast tanks and free flood areas which are outside the pressure hull. These areas also provide the outer hull shape. In addition the forward area holds the sonar sphere and on some submarines the vertical launch tubes for Tomahawk missiles. Inside the pressure hull, the submarine is divided into the other two general areas. Forward of the midships watertight bulkhead (the only one in the boat), are the operational centers, torpedo room, crew and officer quarters and stowage spaces. Aft are the reactor compartment and the engine room which comprise the nuclear propulsion plant.

KEY

1 Rudder
2 Nuclear reactor
3 Control room
4 Weapons loading hatch
5 Electronic equipment space
6 Vertical Launch System
7 Tomahawk missile
8 Forward ballast tank
9 Sonar spherical array
10 Bow planes
11 Torpedo tubes
12 Torpedo room
13 Berthing
14 Deck galley
15 Crew mess
16 Engine room
17 Propulsion machinery
18 After ballast tanks
19 Stern planes

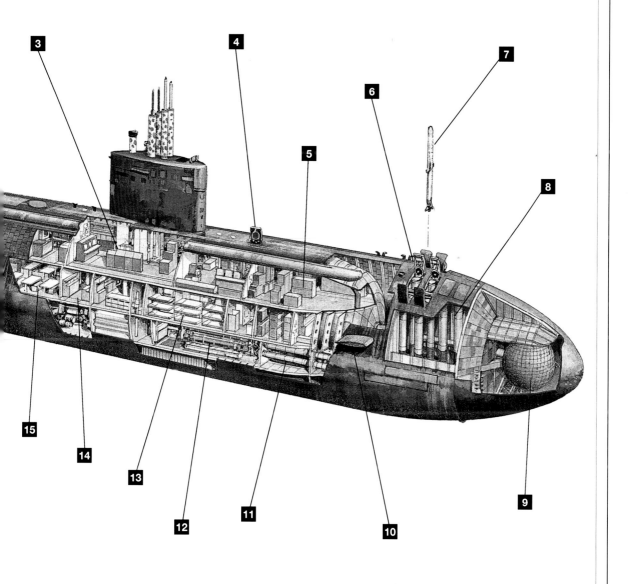

LOS ANGELES CLASS

Class consists 62 ships, USS *Los Angeles* through USS *Cheyenne*

Dimensions Length 360ft; beam 33ft

Displacement (surfaced/submerged) 6,000/6,900 tons

Speed (surfaced/submerged) See author's note

Endurance Only limited by supplies

Design test depth See author's note

Complement (officer/enlisted) 12/115

Armament Torpedo tubes: four Mk 67 (23ft long by 21in. diameter), angled outward from midships. Bow contains sonar spherical array. The tubes and fire-control systems are capable of handling various types of torpedo (Mk 37-3, Mk 37, Mk 48, Mk 48 ADCAP), SubRoc, Harpoon, and Tomahawk missiles. From SSN-619 on, each submarine had a nest of 12 Vertical Launch System (VLS) tubes for the Tomahawk cruise missile.

Service history:

	Laid down	Launched	Commissioned	Decommissioned
USS *Los Angeles* (SSN-688)	8-Jan-72	6-Apr-74	13-Nov-76	–
USS *Baton Rouge* (SSN-689)	18-Nov-72	26-Apr-75	25-Jun-77	13-Jan-95
USS *Philadelphia* (SSN-690)	12-Aug-72	19-Oct-74	25-Jun-77	–
USS *Memphis* (SSN-691)	23-Jun-73	3-Apr-76	21/17/77	–
USS *Omaha* (SSN-692)	27-Jan-73	21-Feb-76	11-Mar-78	5-Oct-95
USS *Cincinnati* (SSN-693)	6-Apr-74	19-Feb-77	10-Jun-78	10-Jun-78
USS *Groton* (SSN-694)	3-Aug-73	9-Oct-76	8-Jul-78	29-Jul-96
USS *Birmingham* (SSN-695)	26-Apr-75	29-Oct-77	16-Dec-78	22-Dec-97
USS *New York City* (SSN-696)	15-Dec-73	18-Jun-77	3-Mar-79	30-Apr-97
USS *Indianapolis* (SSN-697)	19-Oct-74	30-Jul-77	5-Jan-80	22-Dec-98
USS *Bremerton* (SSN-698)	8-May-76	22-Jul-78	28-Mar-81	–
USS *Jacksonville* (SSN-699)	21-Feb-76	18-Nov-78	16-May-81	–
USS *Dallas* (SSN-700)	9-Oct-76	28-Apr-79	18-Jul-81	–
USS *La Jolla* (SSN-701)	16-Oct-76	11-Aug-79	24-Oct-81	–
USS *Phoenix* (SSN-702)	30-Jul-77	8-Dec-79	19-Dec-81	29-Jul-98
USS *Boston* (SSN-703)	11-Aug-78	19-Apr-80	30-Jan-82	19-Nov-99
USS *Baltimore* (SSN-704)	21-May-79	13-Dec-80	24-Jul-82	10-Jul-98
USS *City of Corpus Christi* (SSN-705)	4-Sep-79	25-Apr-81	8-Jan-83	
USS *Albequerque* (SSN-706)	27-Dec-79	13-Mar-82	21-May-83	–
USS *Portsmouth* (SSN-707)	8-May-80	18-Sep-82	1-Oct-83	18-Aug-05
USS *Minneapolis-St. Paul* (SSN-708)	30-Jan-81	19-Mar-83	10-Mar-84	–
USS *Hyman G. Rickover* (SSN-709)	24-Jul-81	27-Aug-83	21-Jul-84	–
USS *Augusta* (SSN-710)	1-Apr-82	21-Jan-84	19-Jan-85	–
USS *San Francisco* (SSN-711)	26-May-77	27-Oct-79	24-Apr-81	–
USS *Atlanta* (SSN-712)	17-Aug-78	16-Aug-80	6-Mar-82	16-Dec-99
USS *Houston* (SSN-713)	29-Jan-79	21-Mar-81	25-Sep-82	–
USS *Norfolk* (SSN-714)	1-Aug-79	31-Oct-81	21-May-83	–
USS *Buffalo* (SSN-715)	25-Jan-80	8-May-82	5-Nov-83	–
USS *Salt Lake City* (SSN-716)	26-Aug-80	16-Oct-82	12-May-84	25-Oct-06
USS *Olympia* (SSN-717)	31-Mar-81	30-Apr-83	17-Nov-83	–
USS *Honolulu* (SSN-718)	10-Nov-81	24-Sep-83	6-Jul-85	1-Nov-06
USS *Providence* (SSN-719)	14-Oct-82	4-Aug-84	27-Jul-85	–
USS *Pittsburgh* (SSN-720)	15-Apr-83	8-Dec-84	23-Nov-85	–
USS *Chicago* (SSN-721)	5-Jan-83	13-Oct-84	27-Sep-86	–
USS *Key West* (SSN-722)	6-Jul-83	20-Jul-85	12-Sep-87	–
USS *Oklahoma City* (SSN-723)	4-Jan-84	2-Nov-85	9-Jul-88	–
USS *Louisville* (SSN-724)	16-Sep-84	14-Dec-85	8-Nov-86	–
USS *Helena* (SSN-725)	28-Mar-85	28-Jun-86	11-Jul-87	–
USS *Newport News* (SSN-750)	3-Mar-84	15-Mar-86	3-Jun-89	–
USS *San Juan* (SSN-751)	16-Aug-85	6-Dec-86	6-Aug-88	–
USS *Pasadena* (SSN-752)	20-May-86	12-Sep-87	11-Feb-89	–
USS *Albany* (SSN-753)	22-Apr-85	13-Jun-87	7-Apr-90	–
USS *Topeka* (SSN-754)	13-May-86	23-Jan-88	21-Oct-88	–
USS *Miami* (SSN-755)	24-Oct-86	12-Nov-88	30-Jun-90	–

	Laid down	Launched	Commissioned	Decommissioned
USS *Scranton* (SSN-756)	29-Aug-86	3-Jul-89	26-Jan-91	–
USS *Alexandria* (SSN-757)	19-Jun-87	23-Jun-90	29-Jun-91	–
USS *Ashville* (SSN-758)	9-Jan-87	28-Oct-89	28-Sep-91	–
USS *Jefferson City* (SSN-759)	21-Sep-87	17-Aug-90	28-Feb-92	–
USS *Annapolis* (SSN-760)	15-Jun-88	18-May-91	11-Apr-92	–
USS *Springfield* (SSN-761)	28-Oct-88	9-Nov-91	4-Dec-92	–
USS *Columbus* (SSN-762)	28-Apr-89	1-Aug-92	24-Jul-93	–
USS *Santa Fe* (SSN-763)	25-May-91	12-Dec-92	8-Jan-94	–
USS *Boise* (SSN-764)	25-Aug-88	23-Mar-91	7-Nov-92	–
USS *Montpelier* (SSN-765)	19-May-89	23-Aug-91	13-Mar-93	–
USS *Charlotte* (SSN-766)	7-Jan-90	3-Oct-92	16-Sep-94	–
USS *Hampton* (SSN-767)	2-Mar-90	3-Apr-92	6-Nov-93	–
USS *Hartford* (SSN-768)	27-Apr-92	4-Dec-94	10-Dec-94	–
USS *Toledo* (SSN-769)	8-Apr-91	28-Aug-93	24-Feb-95	–
USS *Tucson* (SSN-770)	20-Sep-91	19-Mar-94	9-Sep-95	–
USS *Columbia* (SSN-771)	9-Feb-93	24-Sep-94	9-Oct-95	–
USS *Greenville* (SSN-772)	16-Apr-92	17-Sep-94	13-Feb-96	–
USS *Cheyenne* (SSN-773)	6-Oct-92	1-Apr-95	29-Jul-96	–

Those without decommissioning dates are, as of this writing, still in active service.

Los Angeles Class fast attack submarine USS *Alexandria* is submerged after surfacing through two feet of ice during ICEX-07, a US Navy and Royal Navy exercise conducted on and under a drifting ice floe about 180 nautical miles off the north coast of Alaska.

The USS *Seawolf* (SSN-705) underway on the surface, proceeding out of New London on its first sea trials. Lead ship of what would become a 30-ship class, she exceeded all design expectations but proved to be too large and too expensive for a changing world.

Seawolf Class

This class was designed and built to counter the threat of the Soviet navy's new attack submarines, such as the *Alfa* and *Akula*. The fight, if it ever took place, would happen in the deep waters well away from land masses, thus the design was for a "blue-water" system. The 30-boat Seawolf Class was planned as a follow-on to the Los Angeles Class. Larger, faster, and quieter than any of the preceding fast attack classes, the Seawolf sported eight 21-in. torpedo tubes, an extensive integrated sonar/fire-control suite (CCS Mk 2), and a redesigned powerplant complete with a shrouded propulsor. Just as the Seawolf was under construction, the Soviet Union came apart and the world changed. The need for an extensive blue-water submarine force was seen as being over, and the 30 ships of the Seawolf force became only three. Given hull numbers out of sequence, SSN-21, -22, and -23, the class became a testing ground for new concepts and new equipment.

The Seawolf Class exceeded all expectations, albeit at a time when such an expensive and capable boat was considered to be an extravagance by those holding the budgetary purse strings. The upgraded reactor plant and a pumpjet increased the efficiency of the propulsion system. The silencing was also very efficient. These two qualities combined to make the boat very quiet at a high underwater speed. Aside from the USS *Seawolf*, the USS *Connecticut* was completed as a standard Seawolf and the third of the class, the USS *Jimmy Carter*, was extended by nearly 100ft and modified to become a multimission special operations submarine.

A Seawolf class being prepared to move to the graving dock. After the majority of the submarine is built, it is rolled out of the enclosed construction building and onto a barge that sits in a graving dock. The water is then pumped out of the dock until the barge rests on the bottom. When the boat is ready to launch, the dock and barge are then flooded, and the boat floats free for the first time.

SEAWOLF CLASS

Class consists of three ships, USS *Seawolf*, USS *Connecticut*, USS *Jimmy Carter*
Dimensions Length 360ft; beam 40ft; USS *Jimmy Carter* length 453ft
Displacement (surfaced/submerged) 6,000/6,900 tons
Speed (surfaced/submerged) See author's note
Endurance Only limited by supplies
Design test depth See author's note
Complement (officer/enlisted) 12/115
Armament Torpedo tubes: eight torpedo tubes (23ft long by 21in. in diameter). With its exceptionally large torpedo room the boat could carry large numbers of each of the following: Mk 48 ADCAP torpedo, the Harpoon antiship missile, the Tomahawk cruise missile, and Mk 60 CAPTOR (Encapsulated Torpedo) mines.

Virginia Class

A search started in the early 1990s for how to keep the Seawolf Class capabilities yet have a less expensive submarine. The United States submarine force was up against several problems. Many, even in the naval community, saw no further use for a large number of submarines. The Sturgeon Class and early Los Angeles Class boats were reaching the end of their useful lives and hard choices had to be made whether to upgrade these boats in expensive yard overhauls or to decommission

OPPOSITE **A Virginia Class in the construction building at Newport News. The tarp covers protect the fiberglass sonar dome that comprises the bow of the sub. Note the opening in the front of the sail. This houses the upward-looking sonar receiver.**

ABOVE **USS *Virginia* moved out of doors at Groton, Connecticut, August 5, 2003 for the first time in preparation for her christening. Note the bulk of the ship, like an iceberg, is mostly underwater.**

them. The Navy chose the latter. The submarine force was dropping rapidly from a high of nearly 120 submarines toward a number nearer 50, a figure that included the 16 Ohio Class ballistic missile submarines. A new design was undertaken that resulted in a significant change in the way submarines in the US Navy were built and operated.

Two of the driving forces behind this change were the continuing advances in computer technology and the need to reduce the crew of a submarine. Computers were getting better, smaller, and more reliable. A versatile computer network was to be center of the new submarine's electronics design. An outgrowth of this concept was that the submarine's control technology was redesigned as a "fly by wire" computer-assisted system. This system reduced the number of crew actively participating in the helm, planes, ballasting, and trim of the boat, and hence the ship control party was reduced from six to three. Given that the submarine normally operated in a three-watch section daily rotation, the savings in personnel from this change was nine sailors in the crew. This new submarine was to become the Virginia Class.

The first ship of the class marked a new generation of submarine design, construction, and operation. Its sea trials were extraordinary in that, for the first time, there were no major deficiencies noted for correction. The entire vessel was designed using extensive computer visualization and advanced computer aided design (CAD). Seawolf Class had led the way in this new design and build system, but the Virginia Class proved that the system worked on a large scale. The construction method achieved significant savings in cost and manning, and the advanced engineering of the reactor plant meant a great efficiency in fuel loading and use. These submarines will never have to be refueled – the reactor core will last the life of the ship.

Today the US fast attack submarine fleet consists of the Los Angeles Class, which is being replaced by Virginia Class boats as the former reach their end of their useful lives, and two Seawolf Class (the USS *Jimmy Carter* being a special operations boat). The force is more versatile and more capable than ever. They are "always there, never seen."

VIRGINIA CLASS

Class is to consist of 30 ships, and the hull numbers start with SSN-774 and will proceed to SSN-804.

Dimensions Length 377ft; beam 34ft

Displacement (surfaced/submerged) 6,800/7,300 tons

Speed (surfaced/submerged) See author's note

Endurance Only limited by supplies

Design test depth See author's note

Complement (officer/enlisted) 12/115

Armament Weapons suite consists of 12 VLS tubes and four 21-in. torpedo tubes with the capacity for 16 Tomahawk missiles and up to 26 Mk 48 ADCAP torpedoes. The ship is also equipped to carry the Harpoon antiship missile and Mk 60 CAPTOR mines. There is an integral lockout chamber that can host the SEAL Delivery System and SEAL teams for special operations. Sensor and weapons control is via the Command and Control Systems Module (CCSM), which consists of an open architecture grouping of common display and control modules and a modification of the CCS Mk 2 combat system.

Electronic countermeasures include the WLY-1 acoustic countermeasure and the BLQ-10 electronic surveillance system. The sonar system for the Virginia Class consists of the BQQ-10 active and passive spherical array with the low-frequency conformal array in the bow dome. The ship is also fitted with the thick line towed array (TB-29), the thin line towed array, and a wide aperture flank array.

Service history (at time of writing):

	Laid down	Launched	Commissioned
USS *Virginia* (SSN-774)	Sep-99	Aug-03	Oct-04
USS *Texas* (SSN-775)	Jul-02	Apr-05	Sep-06
USS *Hawaii* (SSN-776)	Aug-04	Jun-06	–
USS *New Hampshire* (SSN-777)	May-04	–	–
USS *New Mexico* (SSN-778)	–	–	–

PLATE D

The most modern of the US nuclear fast attack submarines continue the hull form which provides most efficient underwater performance within the constraints of the engineering, habitability, weapons and sensor requirements. Small changes in the outer form can be seen in these three classes. In the Los Angeles Class (1) the sail (fin) is farther aft than is optimal due to the requirement to have the periscopes penetrate directly through the hull to the control room. Electronic-optical (optronic) periscopes which don't use the long optical tube hull penetration have since enabled designers to place the sail (fin) where it will give the most optimal hydrodynamic performance rather than having to be directly over the control room. The Seawolf class (2) was to be a large quiet "blue water" attack submarine to counter the perceived Soviet deep diving fast submarine threat. The open specially shaped screw has given way to the more efficient shrouded propulsor. Seen at the bottom is the Virginia Class (3), which combines the need for a quiet high-speed submarine with the versatility required by today's global military picture.

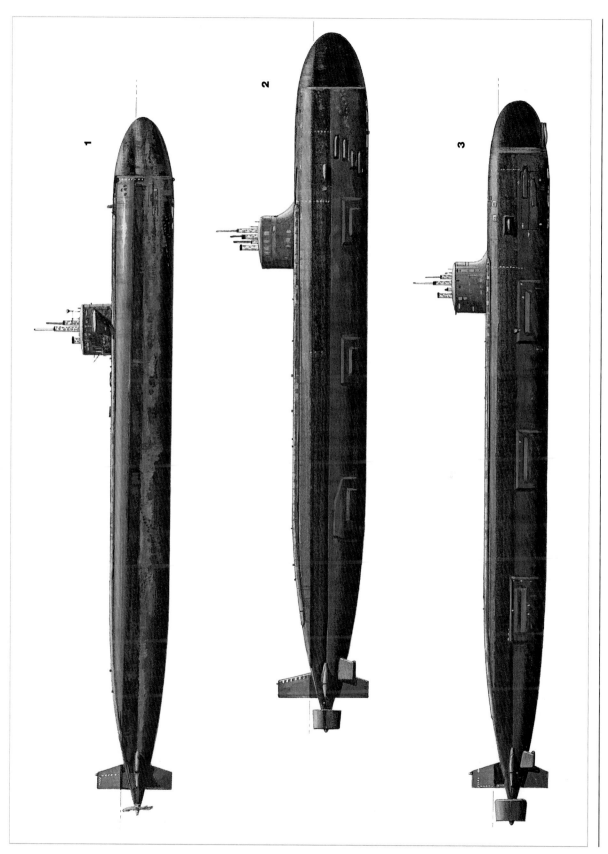

A Virginia Class underway on trials. Extending from the top of the sail are two BRA-34 antennae, a snorkel mast, and a multipurpose ESM antenna. Aft of the sail is the open hatch to the operations compartment, with the man handing down the last of the items topside. He will then drop down and seal the hatch, completing the topside "Rig for Dive."

FAST ATTACK SUBMARINE SENSORS

Submarine systems do not develop and evolve in a vacuum. In most cases advances in the technology of one system impacts on each of the other systems in the boat. The submarine is an integrated weapons platform that depends on the capabilities of all its technologies. As sonars became more powerful and were able to analyze a wider spectrum of noise, for example, the requirement for submarine silencing grew. Equally, as the capabilities of the onboard computer systems grew it became possible to analyze noise faster and more accurately. It became possible to compute the paths that noise took through the water. It was found that there were sound channels in which noise traveled relatively unchanged. There were also areas where sound paths curved deep and came back up to the surface, were reflected, curved deep, and reappeared (these became known as convergence zones). Predicting these paths and zones in existing ocean conditions became an important part of the sonar's task.

The increase in computer power also drove advances in Electronic Surveillance Measures (ESM) sensors as they became more able to analyze a wider electronic spectrum with greater speed and detail. As electronics devices became smaller and more capable, antennae and masts could have combined functions. For example, as far back as World War II simple radar antennae were mounted in the upper head of periscopes. The periscopes have evolved to take on more and more functions and an increasing number of antennae are mounted in their upper ends. Weapons also drove fire-control system and sonar development. As the fire-control systems became more capable, the torpedo in turn became "smarter." The early Mk 14 torpedo could be compared with an air-launched "dumb bomb" or "iron bomb." The Mk 37, however, had a hydrophone in its nose and could seek out its target as it got closer, making it more likely to achieve hits. In addition, it was wire guided.

Sonar consoles on USS *Thresher*. This set of active/passive sonar inboard electronics comprised the BQS-6/BQA-3 sonar. The active sonar console is in the middle with the passive on the left and the BQA-3 graphic indicator on the right. The man in the photo, Sonarman First Class R. E. Steinel, was aboard *Thresher* when it was lost.

As computers and sonar systems became smaller, a computer could be put into the torpedo so that through a wire-guidance system the onboard fire-control computer could talk directly to the torpedo. There was a spool of thin wire connecting the torpedo with the torpedo tube, and the wire was used to send a signal to the torpedo once it was launched. The course of the torpedo was altered as needed if updated information showed the existing fire-control solution was in error or the target had made some radical maneuver. In addition, the torpedo could be programmed with the acoustic signature of the selected target and become a "fire and forget" weapon – the Mk 48 ADCAP (advanced capability) is such a torpedo. Therefore, in the discussion of the technologies below, one should view the items evolving as an entire group rather than individual systems.

When submerged a submarine must rely on sensors to navigate, locate targets, prosecute an attack, communicate, perform surveillance and accomplish any other assigned tasks. For convenience these sensors may be grouped into the following categories: sonar, electronic surveillance, radar, navigation, communications, and optical.

Sonar

The electrical signal output of the hydrophone can be processed in several ways. The simplest is to look at the signal with respect to time, as through an oscilloscope, a process called time series analysis. It is, however, more useful to look at the intensity level at a particular frequency. To do this the signal is passed through a set of filters that only allow through the frequency of interest. This method allows the operator to listen for a particular noise – for example, the known frequency of a particular piece of machinery in an enemy ship. The selection of filters to select noise signals is used in an analog system. A digital system can sample a noise signal many times per second and convert each sample into a number which can be plugged into a set of equations to derive more information from the signal faster and more accurately than an analog system. The level of the signal is stored as a number that can be processed by a computer. The mathematical process generally used to perform the analysis is a Fourier Transform, and early computers performed this function using software and what is called a Fast Fourier Transform (FFT). As computers evolved, the processing also evolved into being hardwired in integrated circuits called digital signal processors (DSP).

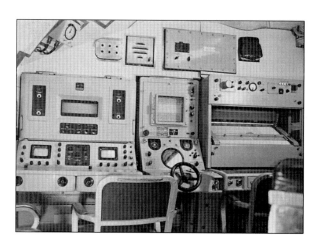

The BQR-7 system of sonar consoles.

The hydrophone is a simple device that listens "all around." When multiple hydrophones are placed together and linked with electrical devices called delay lines, the array can discriminate in the direction it listens, something generally called "beamforming." US Navy sonar systems are designated by a multiple letter number system. The first letter is the installation type ("B" for submarine), the second is the equipment type ("Q" for sonars), and the third is the equipment's purpose ("R" for receiving, meaning in the case of sonar the passive elements, and "S" for sending or the active portions). Finally there is a number to designate the specific equipment. Thus BQR-7 is a submarine passive sonar. The following is a very general description of the sonar types as they evolved through the various fast attack submarines.

The *Nautilus* up through the Skipjacks had a form of the BQR-4 and BQS-7 system. This was a system that used electronic beamforming through switches and analog filters to transmit active and receive passive information. The information was displayed on electronic screens and on scrolling paper plots. Tracking information was fed directly to the fire-control system in the form of bearing to the target. In the Permit Class several sonar arrays were combined and the system was generally designated the

The BQQ-5 integrated console. This console, along with several other identical ones, constitute the entire sonar suite, and was standard equipment on Los Angeles Class and was backfitted onto some Sturgeon Class. (Author's photograph: Submarine Force Library and Museum)

BQQ-1, the second "Q" meaning "combined" or "special." The advent of computers capable of performing the digital filtering of the noise signal meant the signal could be analyzed faster and with more resolution. The Sturgeons received the BQQ-3 (which was backfitted to the Permits) – it was essentially a sonar system that not only used all-digital tracking and filtering, but featured the BQR-20 spectrum analyzer, which could display the noise signal in an X-Y graph display, the noise level on the vertical axis and the frequencies on the horizontal axis. This system was coupled with a library of existing spectral plots of known signals of interest (read this to mean known target signatures).

In the early days sonar depended on the ears and knowledge of the operator to discriminate the noise of a target from all the other noise in the ocean. The advances in sonar systems were generally directed at both extracting more information from the noise and quantifying the noise so it was not so dependent on the operator. The ability to analyze the level (loudness) of the noise at each of many discrete frequencies meant that the sound produced by an external source (such as a target ship) could be quantified as a specific noise signature. As the system became more accurate and faster, new analytical methods were introduced, such as Doppler analysis. Doppler is the frequency shift in a moving object – higher if it is closing, lower if it is moving away. As the hydrophone arrays became larger and the technology of hydrophones advanced, the accuracy of the bearing to the target improved. The result was an increase in the accuracy of Target Motion Analysis (TMA). TMA is vital to the "all passive sonar" approach to the fire-control problem and allows a more accurate fire-control solution. All the systems described improve the ability of the submarine to detect a target early and at long range, accurately identify the target, separate its signature from those contacts that may not be hostile, and determine what the target is doing in real time.

Some of the sonar arrays are:

Spherical Array – This array is located inside the bow sonar dome. It consists of a steel sphere about 16ft in diameter in the Permit Class to 24ft in the Virginia Class. On the outside of the sphere is a closely packed collection of hydrophones, each pointed out from the center so each hydrophone listens in a different direction.

34 | **Conformal Array** – Here a set of relatively widely spaced hydrophones are mounted inside the bow dome and generally conform to the shape of the dome curve. It is designed for detecting low-frequency noise.

Wide Aperture Array – Located in three places along each side of the submarine are planar arrays. These are used to achieve rapid passive ranging to a target.

Towed Array Sonar – A set of hydrophones in a linear array is towed on the end of a cable, which can be unreeled to a length of over 1,000ft. This array is therefore behind the turbulent area created by the submarine's hull and propulsion. There are two types of towed array in use. The TB-29 is called the thin-line towed array and the TB-16 the thick-line towed array.

Spot Hydrophones – Single hydrophones are sited at various places around the hull in free flood spaces and ballast tanks. These monitor the noise created by machinery inside the hull and are used to determine the ambient noise level around the ship.

Sail Front Array – In this case there is an active and passive sonar array set (BQS-15 and Mine and Ice Detection Active Sonar, MIDAS) mounted on the front of the sail and under the forefoot. These arrays are used for looking upward and for under-ice and minefield navigation.

Threat Detection Array – At various points on the ship small arrays are mounted, specifically tuned to detect the noise of threats such as torpedoes. These are collectively known as the WLR-1 through -9 and the WLY-1 acoustic intercept systems

Electronic surveillance

One of the most useful tasks performed by fast attack submarines during the Cold War was that of electronic surveillance. This consisted of using a variety of mast-mounted antennae coupled with a system that could analyze the electronic signals being received. The ESM looked at the electromagnetic spectrum in much the same way a sonar system looked at the noise field in the water. Early systems used analog filters to discriminate frequencies. Some antennae were moved into the tops of periscopes. As digital systems became standard, computer-driven analysis systems took over. The capabilities of each of the systems, however, are closely held secrets.

Radar

Fast attack submarines carry a radar system not unlike that carried by many commercial vessels of a similar size. It is generally used for navigation only, although it can be used for fire control and to provide a warning of airborne and surface threats under certain circumstances. However, radar is not a passive system, and a submarine that uses it broadcasts its position. Today the standard radar system is the mast mounted BPS-15.

Navigation

Several systems are used to determine the ship's position accurately. These have changed during the evolution of the nuclear fast attack submarine. On board *Nautilus*, navigation was by star sight, sun lines, Omni, Loran (both using shore-based radio stations), and dead reckoning – good enough for the time, but not good enough for the tasks ahead. The Ships Inertial Navigation System (SINS) was developed for the accurate position keeping needed for ballistic missile submarines, and its technology was modified to fit in fast attacks. The first satellite navigation system used the time signal of passing navigation satellites. The signal could be quickly received by sticking up an antenna. SINS was further downsized by using laser ring gyros, and increased computer power allowed many of the large cabinets to be eliminated. Today, the navigation systems consist of specialized inertial navigation coupled with the Global Positioning System (GPS). The submarine force is changing to the Electronic Chart Display Information System (ECDIS), which will eliminate the need for paper chart navigation.

Communications

Secure radio communication is vital for a fast attack. Its technology can be inferred, but security classification makes it seriously difficult to discuss accurately, and justly so. The systems have evolved from high-speed encrypted teletype transmissions to digital bursts to comms using orbiting satellites. For a long time, the Extremely Low Frequency (ELF) communication from giant antennae worked very well. The submarine could receive this data at a relatively shallow depth – a buoyant wire was trailed behind the sub, and this system might still be in use. The Virginia Class can receive information from many sources, even the internet.

Part of the Mk 113 fire-control system. This hybrid analog/digital system replaced the Mk 101 system that was the mainstay during the latter part of World War II and into the late 1950s. The system provided solutions for the torpedo shoot and was also used to fire the SubRoc missile. (Author's photograph: Submarine Force Library and Museum)

Periscopes

The Virginia Class has, as standard equipment, the non-penetrating periscope, which is solely electronic in its image acquisition. The periscope does not penetrate the pressure hull, thus simplifying interior design of the operating spaces because the location of the control room is no longer defined by the scopes. This new device can acquire image data in a wider range of frequencies than the human eye and sends this data to computer memory for review.

THE FIRE-CONTROL SYSTEM AND WEAPONS

A submarine fire-control system is a grouping of equipment that is tasked or designed to solve a complex relative motion problem. The idea is to fire a torpedo or missile that will intersect with the path of a target at the exact time the target reaches a particular spot. The problem is mathematical in nature, with a set of known variables and a set of unknown variables. The problem must be solved in real time. The variables can be further divided by three influences – those belonging to your ship (called "own ship"), those belonging to the weapon, in most cases a torpedo, and those belonging to the target.

Own ship variables are all known and consist of position, course and speed (which come from the onboard gyroscope and pitometer log), and

Loading a SubRoc Missile. The missile is being slid athwartships to align it with a torpedo tube on a Permit Class submarine. Note the restricted space in which to handle and conduct maintenance on the weapons. SubRoc was a submarine-launched rocket that was capable of carrying a nuclear warhead. Its use was limited and it was phased out and is no longer on submarines.

depth (from onboard depth gauges). The weapon's variables are also known and consist of the weapon's speed, any turns that may be programmed into the weapon, and its running depth. The variables belonging to the target are mostly unknown and must be determined by various means. The method most familiar to the public – the use of a periscope to spot and track a target – went by the wayside after World War II. Thereafter, sonar became the primary means of supplying the target information that would enable the fire-control system to make the target's unknowns into knowns. A fire-control system generally works by making a prediction and correction solution. The own ship's information and that of the torpedo are continuously fed into the fire-control computer, as is the information from the sonar about the target's bearing. The target's speed, range, and depth are approximated from information such as the target's capabilities and its screw speed. The fire-control computer then predicts what the bearing will be at some future time, correcting that prediction with new information. The prediction is computed over and over as fast as possible until the predicted bearing matches the actual bearing. At this point the fire-control system alerts the operators that a solution had been reached, and the weapon can be launched.

As the nuclear fast attack submarine evolved in engineering and technology, so did the fire-control system. *Nautilus* used a system not unlike that used on World War II fleet submarines. It was an electro-mechanical system that applied a complex system of syncros, servos, gearing, and cams to solve the relative motion problem. This system was relatively slow and had difficulty keeping up with the increased speed of the submarine and its supposed targets. Through the early 1960s the systems became more electrical and less mechanical, with increased use of hardwired analog computers. As advances in the fire-control system occurred, the new systems were installed on submarines being built, and backfitted where possible onto older boats.

The Mk 113 was a hybrid system that had not only the analog elements but also a hardwired digital computer. Ballistic missile submarines made use of the Mk 84 digital computer for missile firing, and that system's capabilities were carried over to the fast attack submarine's Mk 113 system. As the power of programmable digital computers increased while their size decreased, they took over more

The SubRoc was the first and only submarine-launched long-range nuclear-armed antisubmarine missile ever deployed by the US Navy. An enemy submarine had virtually no chance of escaping a SubRoc, especially since its sonar could not detect the missile in the air.

of the mathematics from the electro-mechanical and analog systems. By the time the Los Angeles Class was into its full-up build cycle, the new Mk 117, an all-digital programmable fire-control system, was introduced and first installed on the USS *Dallas* (SSN-700). It was backfitted on most existing submarines and became the standard system until nearly the end of the Los Angeles Class' build cycle. The Mk 117 system underwent a significant upgrade with the adoption of the Over The Horizon Targeting (OTH-T) that would be used for the Harpoon antiship missile and the Tomahawk cruise missile. The OTH-T substituted radio flash messages for onboard sensors in supplying information on the target to the fire-control system. About the same time the ship's sonar systems changed from analog to digital computing with the installation of the BQQ-5 sonar system. Because the sonar and fire-control systems were now both fully digital there was a design effort to combine the systems into an integrated sonar/fire-control system.

The weapons suite for fast attack submarines is listed in the table below:

Weapon designator	Type	Range	Speed (kts)	Warhead	Applicability (Class)	Remarks
Mk 14 Mod 3	Torpedo	4,500–9,000yd	35–50	668lb TPX	Nautilus to Skipjack	WWII mainstay torpedo, in service until late 1970s
Mk 16 Mod 1–8	Torpedo	11,000yd	40	960lb TPX	Nautilus to Skipjack	Used NAVOL fuel (hydrogen peroxide), withdrawn 1978
Mk 27	Torpedo	6,000yd	40	900lb TPX	Nautilus to Permit	Electric (storage battery) propulsion, replaced by Mk 37
Mk 37 Mods 1, 3	Torpedo	8,000–18,000yd	Various	330lb HBX-3	Nautilus to Los Angeles	Homing and wire guided. Also in NT Mk37E
Mk 45	Torpedo	30,000–40,000yd	Various	Nuclear Capable	Skate to Sturgeon	In service 1957 to 1976, called ASTOR
Mk 48	Torpedo	30,000–40,000yd	Various	800lb HBX-3	Permit to Los Angeles	Wire guided, homing and pattern running, Uses OTTO monopropellant
Mk 48 ADCAP	Torpedo	30,000–40,000yd	Various	800lb HBX-3	Permit to Virginia	Wire guided, homing and pattern running, Uses OTTO monopropellant, built to counter the deep diving Soviet submarines.
SubRoc UUM-44	Rocket	30nm	N/A	Nuclear Capable	Permit to Los Angeles	ASW weapon prior to advent of Mk-48 torpedo
Harpoon (UGM-84A/C)	Antiship Missile	75nm	600	488lb WDU-18	Sturgeon to Virginia	Submarine version of a versatile standoff antiship weapon.
Tomahawk BGM-109B/C	Cruise Missile	250–1,350nm	500	700–1,000lb	Sturgeon to Virginia	Modern multipurpose weapon. Speed and range is warhead dependent
Special operations	SEAL Teams	N/A	N/A	N/A	Sturgeon to Virginia	Descendent from UDT teams of WWII.

PLATE E

The nuclear fast attack submarine is fitted with a variety of weapons from torpedoes to missiles. At the top is a Mark 37 Mod 3 torpedo, which was an antisubmarine and anti-escort weapon. It was wire guided and had an acoustic homing feature. It evolved into the Mark 48 ADCAP that has become the mainstay torpedo in the US submarine fleet. Not only wire guided and fast, it has enough computing power aboard and enough of a sophisticated acoustic homing (passive and active) feature to be a "fire and forget" weapon. The white SubRoc between the two was an interim weapon to counter the threat of large Soviet submarine numbers. It was nuclear capable but is no longer carried. The Tomahawk cruise missile can be launched from torpedo tubes or on the submarines so equipped with the VLS. With terrain following and GPS navigation systems, a range of over 1,200nm, and a warhead of over 500lb of high explosive, it is an extremely formidable stand-off weapon. Below that is a portrayal of the Harpoon antiship missile as it breaks the surface and heads off to its assigned target. This view is often the first indication an enemy has that there is a US fast attack submarine in the area.

HISTORY AND OPERATIONAL USE

A word is necessary here about Admiral Hyman Rickover. His name has become synonymous with the United States naval nuclear power program. In fact, it is commonly believed that he personally designed the nuclear propulsion plants. The admiral was a brilliant engineer, but more than that he was also a brilliant manager. He saw that in order to build and maintain a safe and effective nuclear propulsion system in the Navy, certain things had to happen outside the realm of actual system design. Perceiving that there were inherent dangers in the use of nuclear reactors, he set in motion changes in the way the submarine navy (and later on the surface fleet) did business. Fleet submarine systems were simple enough that operations and maintenance were done on the basis of "corporate knowledge," with minimal use of technical documentation. The senior petty officers supervised this maintenance and passed on their expertise to their juniors. The worst that could happen if an error was made was some deranged equipment or less than optimal operations. However, the nuclear reactor made the "worst case condition" much worse – the concept of an accident took on a whole new meaning. To counter the danger, Admiral Rickover set in motion a strict regimen of operation and maintenance. Documentation was created that set forth how the plant was to be operated and how maintenance was to be performed. This documentation was to be followed precisely. Technical training was codified and intensified. Nuclear powerplant operators (colloquially called "nucs" – pronounced nooks) had training on the actual powerplants after their initial technical training as machinists, electricians, and so on. The training was intense and tended to weed out all but the most dedicated and capable operators. In addition, Admiral Rickover extended the reach of this quest for excellence to the shipyards that built the subs and the contractors and vendors that supplied materials for the construction and maintenance of the boats. His requirements were written into the specifications and contracts. Only those who could meet the specs did business with the Navy. This meant that that there was full accountability from the vendor who supplied the parts through to the operator who used the parts and everywhere in between. That the nuclear propulsion plants in US submarines have such a good safety record and are perceived by the general public to be safe is the legacy of "The Admiral."

In order to allow personnel to pass through the reactor compartment safely, a narrow passage was part of the design of all fast attacks. The tunnel was shielded against the types of radiation expected from the reactor and its attendant systems, thus allowing a safe transit through the compartment.

This is one of the Los Angeles Class that has bow planes instead of sail planes, and it sports a 12-tube VLS from which Tomahawk missiles are fired. The sail is also hardened to be able to punch through the Arctic ice.

What did fast attacks do?

It's April 2, 1991, and it's dark outside. In the control room of the USS *Pittsburgh* (SSN-720), however, it's blue, red, amber, and green. The blue is from the lights that during the day would be white, but which now are rigged for night and cast a relatively dim blue aura over everything. The other colors come from indicator lights, sonar displays, and computer screens. The crew is at battle stations. They have been to battle stations nearly daily for the past month.

Los Angeles Class boat in dry dock. Proper maintenance and repair is vital if a submarine is to keep its operational commitments. All bases have either access to naval shipyards with dry docks and/or floating dry docks, such as are shown here. With the boat completely out of the water, work on the underside and on hull valves can be accomplished.

Modern submarines are built specifically to travel completely submerged – their round hulls with no rolling chocks and their low bridges make them miserable in any significant seaway. This photo is of a Skipjack Class boat, which had the highest of all the fast attack sails, trying to make a high-speed surface run.

The boat is deep in the dark confines of the Red Sea. However, this day, the battle stations would be different. Instead of being practice and training, what was to happen would be real. There was a certain tension in the air and a lack of some of the banter that might be present during practice runs. The officer supervising the fire-control stations makes a report to the captain that the required targeting package has been entered into the Tomahawk missiles that reside in the launch tubes at the forward end of the boat. The captain acknowledges this information then orders the boat to proceed to launch depth. The sonar supervisor calls out the changes in the contacts held by the sonar system. He ensures the surface of the water is clear of any intrusive ships and that no hostile submarines are lurking. In a manner similar to that seen in the movies, the captain calls out, "Firing point procedures." Procedure manuals are already open to the proper pages and checkoff sheets are at hand. The control-room personnel do all the things that are listed. The tubes are ready, the missiles are ready, the ship's position is proper, and the crew is prepared. The captain orders "Tube one, SHOOT." Buttons are pressed and the boat gives a slight shudder. The fire-control system supervisor announces, "Missile away, tube one." In the night sky above the submerged submarine, the missile breaks the surface, its booster ignites, and the calm waters are lit with an eerie light. The missile arcs away and heads for its intended target – downtown Baghdad's Iraqi command-and-control center. Operation *Desert Shield* has just become *Desert Storm* and the air war has begun. The missiles were part of the initial effort to silence the Iraqi air defense. It is not the only time that Tomahawks have suddenly and without warning burst from a quiet ocean and headed off for a distant target. One of the advantages of a submarine is that it can lurk unseen off the coast and reach out over 1,200 miles to put a warhead on a target. It has been said that the attack launched by the USS *Pittsburgh* and the USS *Louisville* on that April morning was singularly successful.

The above description is an approximation because the actual records are classified. The operational logs for all US Navy nuclear fast attack submarines are kept on the ship, or if the ship is decommissioned at the National Archives and Records Administration (NARA). In any case, these logs are classified and unobtainable for the general researcher. Some tidbits of information have become public, however, but the evidence, although from reputable sources, is anecdotal for the most part. What is evident, though, is the importance of the role played by the fast attack submarine in the Cold War.

After World War II the United States and its allies had to keep close tabs on the Soviet navy and learn about the environs of the Barents and North Pacific areas. Starting in 1949, submarines of the US Navy (and presumably others) ventured into these areas to conduct oceanographic research to learn about everything from sonar conditions to the ability to communicate by radio in the far north. At first these operations were carried out by diesel-electric subs. They set up early-warning "barrier patrols" and watched for a possible "breakout" of the Soviet navy around the North Cape and down through the Greenland, Iceland, United Kingdom (GIUK) gaps in the Atlantic and out around the Kirules and down past Tshima Straits in the Pacific. As the nuclear fast attack submarines came on line they took over these tasks, maintaining a continuous presence outside all the Soviet naval ports. The surveillance took on more and more rigorous tasks as the abilities of the boats were tested and advanced. Acoustic and electronic signatures were taken and recorded, deployment times and patterns were observed,

even photos of the undersides of Soviet naval vessels were taken and vessels followed. These actions were rolled out on a continuous basis, 24 hours a day, every day. For the last four decades of the 20th century and into the present century, the fast attack submarine has kept a non-stop watch.

ABOVE **A fast attack submarine on the surface provides little in the way of freeboard or a safe deck to work upon. The sail doesn't stick up very far and in a moderate seaway is wet. To surface and attempt any useful work such as a rescue at sea is difficult at best and highly dangerous.**

After the collapse of the Soviet Union several high-ranking Soviet naval officers have stated that this continuous presence of silent, unobserved submarines was a significant reason for the end of the communist regime. It is a very real fact that the invisible presence of fast attack submarines figures highly in the military thinking of nearly every country, especially as those submarines can launch high-explosive weapons that have a range of over 1,000 miles and aiming systems that can pick which floor of a building to hit. This ability was proven several times before and during the *Desert Storm* battle and in the conflicts of post-9/11. In this world of new types of conflict, the standard view of a submarine – its periscope sticking up attacking a convoy of enemy ships – is as dated as ships of the line

BELOW **Los Angeles Class submarines can be quickly adapted to dock the Deep Submergence Rescue Vessel (DSRV) and carry it to the scene of a submarine in distress. Here the USS *La Jolla* (SSN-701) has been fitted with the rescue vehicle *Mystic* (DSRV-1) for submarine rescue exercises.**

meeting in a yardarm-to-yardarm fight. The role of the modern submarine in today's world is being debated by naval experts all over the world and the jury is out.

Rescue operations

Some little-known and unusual events that have become public present a different face of the fast attack submarine. First to set the scene. A fast attack submarine is at home in the deep. It is a round-bottomed vessel with good longitudinal stability, but "rolls like a drunken pig" when on the surface on any

PLATE F
One of the more interesting tasks assigned to nuclear fast attack submarines during the Cold War was following a Soviet warship, many times a submarine, to acquire information as to its acoustic signature and its operational methods. This task, called "trailing" meant many days of intense concentration by the trailing submarine's crew. Shown here is a Sturgeon Class US submarine following a Soviet Victor III which has just made a sharp turn to port. This maneuver was performed at random intervals so the submarine could check the area directly behind it in an area called the "baffles." This area is masked from the ship's sonar by not only the sonar's position (in the bow) but by the turbulence set up by the submarine's screw. The maneuver is called "clearing the baffles" but has been popularized in books and movies as the "crazy Ivan" maneuver.

seaway. The only saving grace is that they have one hatch open to the bridge and take little water, if any, into the interior. But the time they spend on the surface is minimal and, in general, submariners have little time to obtain "sea legs." Two fast attack submarines, however, have performed exemplary rescues at sea in severe storms.

On July 8, 1972, the USS *Barb* (SSN-596), alongside in Apra Harbor, Guam, and nearly ready to get underway, received an "operational immediate" message. A B-52 bomber, call-sign Cobalt 2, had gone down at sea some 300 miles from Guam. All ships were to proceed to the area to effect a rescue. There were two submarines that could respond quickly. One, the USS *Gurnard* (SSN-662), was underway transiting from Japan and was nearing Guam. The *Barb* was the other. Within an hour *Barb* was underway and just outside the harbor it submerged to make best possible speed to the crash area. Things were quiet below while the submarine sped to the scene. As it drew closer Commander Jergens, captain of the *Barb*, slowly brought the boat from the depths toward the surface. The crew had rescue equipment at the ready in the control room and had reviewed the

The Los Angeles Class fast attack submarine USS *Dallas* (SSN 700) heads to sea following a brief port visit. *Dallas* is the first Los Angeles Class submarine to have a dry deck shelter. Dry deck shelters provide specially configured nuclear-powered submarines with a greater capability of deploying Special Operations Forces.

rescue plan they were to implement. As they came toward the surface the boat started to roll more and more. A storm had reached typhoon strength, forcing all the possible surface-ship rescuers to run for cover lest they also needed rescue. *Gurnard* was still too far away, so *Barb* became the B-52 crewmen's only hope. Ten degrees rolling each way became 20 then 30 and grew more as the boat surfaced. The captain tried to find a course that would both close on the raft and minimize the rolling. Heading into the sea was not an option because the bridge, only 15ft off the water in a calm sea, was forced under when the boat ran under an oncoming wave. An orbiting aircraft dropped other rafts and flares to direct the submarine to the survivors. Inside the boat the crewmen, not used to the rough weather, were sick, thrown about, and generally miserable, but their thoughts were not only on their own safety but the rescue of their fellows adrift in the massive storm. Just after eight in the morning the bridge was again manned and other members of the rescue team rigged lifelines on the fairwater planes. With the raft being blown nearer and nearer, Jergens made an upwind approach and shotlines were fired to the survivors. However, these thin lines broke again and again. Chief Heintz, on the

PLATE G

One of the tasks performed by nuclear fast attacks is one they are ill equipped for. However, when called upon, they will race to a scene to attempt a surface rescue of those in "peril on the sea." One such rescue was performed by the USS *Scamp* (SSN-588). In the cold North Atlantic the boat answered the call to rescue sailors in distress. She surfaced in the middle of the storm to try to help. Being round bottomed and short, the Skipjack Class submarine is ill suited for surface operations and the sailors inside are not used to rough seas. The submarine's crew fastened everything inside down and prepared for a rough ride. Surfacing near the liferaft she tried to get a line over. The seas were slamming against the sail, one wave tearing off the access door over the sail planes. Finally one of the crewmen from the sinking Panamanian freighter was rescued. Unfortunately he was the only one to survive.

bridge with the captain and the officer of the deck, volunteered to swim to the raft to assist in the rescue. Between Heintz and Petty Officer Spaulding (who was one of the more muscular of the *Barb*'s crew), a heavier line was put across and the actual rescue started. One of the airmen had broken his arm in the ejection, and was first to be hauled up. Spaulding held onto the rescue safety line and as the boat rolled one way pulled it in quickly. As the boat rolled the other his strong arms plucked the airman from the water like a fish on a line. Soon all the crew were deposited in the control room and carried down to the crew's mess, where the corpsman awaited to deal with injuries and any other problems. *Gurnard* had now arrived on the scene and was commencing a rescue attempt on the plane's captain, who was in another raft. The 70-mile-per-hour winds and 30ft-plus seas were playing havoc with her attempt to get in position. Finally, after hours of being vectored by aircraft to the other raft, *Gurnard* plucked the last survivor from the sea. So in addition to the surveillance, trailing, and myriad other operations over the 50-year history of the nuclear fast attack, rescue at sea can be added to the list of accomplishments.

During the rescue by USS *Scamp*, the doors that lead from the inside of the sail to the sail planes were torn completely off by the fury of the waves.

Where did they all go?

When a submarine reaches the end of its useful life, it is decommissioned in a formal ceremony. The national ensign and commissioning pennant are taken down and the crew departs the ship. Then comes the process known as the Submarine Recycling Program (SRP). The boat is placed in a dry dock and the reactor core is removed. The entire reactor compartment is then cut out intact. The core is transported to the Navy's radioactive waste storage facility in Idaho and the reactor compartment is sealed and barged to a storage facility in Hanford, Washington. The ship is then stripped. All useable parts such as electronics and habitability items are stored for immediate reuse. Wiring and cables are pulled out to recycle for their copper. Hull and piping steel is cut up for reuse. This steel, along with other metal structures and piping, is of a high quality and is much valued. All the parts and material that can be recycled or salvaged in any way are separated, sorted, and shipped off to the appropriate facility.

This photo, taken in the early 1990s, shows the reactor compartment storage trench in Hanford, WA. This will be the final resting place for submarine reactor compartments until the radioactivity level drops far enough to allow the metal to be recycled. That will be a long time from now. This trench is now nearly full.

The submarine is then slowly taken apart until nothing is left but the records and the memories. In some cases, however, parts are preserved in memorials and museums. Sail structures in particular are sought after as parts of museum complexes. In Groton, CT, for example, as a part of the Naval Submarine Museum is the sail of the USS *George Washington*, the first ballistic missile submarine.

Fast attack submarines of the US Navy have a long and proud career. They continue to be sailed by highly professional men who see their job as vital in the maintenance of peace and the lynchpin of the United States' global naval strength. Always ready, always there, never seen.

A Los Angeles Class submarine with a dry deck shelter on the after deck. This served as a lockout chamber for SEALs and was accessed from inside the boat through the operations compartment hatch. The shelter could house the SEAL team equipment and a SEAL delivery vehicle.

BIBLIOGRAPHY

For an overview of the nuclear submarine and its people:

Gillcrist, Dan, *Power Shift: The Transition to Nuclear Power in the U.S. Submarine Force As Told by Those Who Did It*, iUniverse, Lincoln, NE (2006)

Rockwell, Theodore, *The Rickover Effect: How One Man Made a Difference*, iUniverse, Lincoln, NE (2002)

Navy SEALs conduct a fast-rope exercise from the cargo door of an HH-60 "Seahawk" assigned to Helicopter Anti-Submarine Squadron Seven on the hull of the fast attack submarine USS *Hampton* in August 1998.

For some of what was done:

Sontag, Sherry, Christopher Drew, Annette Lawrence Drew, *Blind Man's Bluff: The Untold Story of American Submarine Espionage*, Public Affairs, New York (1998)

Weir, Gary E. and Walter J. Boyne, *Rising Tide: The Untold Story of the Russian Submarines That Fought the Cold War*, Basic Books, New York (2003)

On the technical side:

Friedman, Norman, *Naval Institute Guide to World Naval Weapon Systems*, Naval Institute Press, Annapolis, MD (1989)

Friedman, Norman, and James L. Christley, *U.S. Submarines Since 1945: An Illustrated Design History*, Naval Institute Press, Annapolis, MD (1994)

Polmar, Norman, and K. J. Moore, *Cold War Submarines: The Design and Construction of U.S. and Soviet Submarines, 1945–2001*, Brassey's, Washington, DC (2004)

INDEX

Figures in **bold** refer to illustrations. Plates are shown with page locators in brackets.

air conditioning 8, 9, **16**
Albacore, USS 12, **13**
Alexandria, USS (SSN-757) **27**
antennae 32, **22**, **32**

ballast tank blow systems 18–19
Barb, USS (SSN-596) 44–46
Barbel, USS 12
Barbel Class **14**, **B1** (15)
Blueback, USS 12
Bonefish, USS 12
bow planes **9**, **40**
Bureau of Ships (BuShips) 5, 21

Caudle, Carson W. **13**
clearing the baffles **F** (43)
Clifford, Clark 22
Cold War 41–42, **F** (42)
Columbia, USS (SSN-771) **22**
combat-control systems 23, 27, 29
communications 36
Comstock, Commodore 5
Connecticut, USS 28, 30
construction methods
    computer-aided 30
    CONFORM (Concept Formulation) process 22
Crazy Ivan maneuver **F** (43)

Dallas, USS (SSN-700) 39, **44**
decommissioning and disposal 46
design: computer-aided 30
Doppler analysis 34
dry deck shelters **44**, **47**

electronic surveillance 35
    ESM antennae **32**

fairwater planes 21, 23
Fast Fourier Transform (FFT) 33
fire-control systems 23, 27, 29, 36–39, 41

Gertier, Morton **13**
graving docks 28
Guppy (Greater Underwater Propulsion Program) 4
Gurnard, USS (SSN-662) 44, 46

Hampton, USS (SSN-767) **47**
hatches **5**
Heintz, Chief 44–46
helicopters **47**
Holland, USS (SS-1) 11, **12**
hull design
    body of revolution 11–12, **12**, **13**, **B** (15)
    diesel-electric submarines 3–4
    early nuclear submarines **A** (7), 10
    internal frames **16**
    Los Angeles Class **C** (24–25)
    most modern **D** (31)
    Sturgeon Class 19
hydrophones 4, 33, 35
hydroplanes 12, **14**

ice: moving through **3**, **21**, **27**, **40**

Jergens, Commander 44
Jimmy Carter, USS 28, 30

launching **22**, **28**
logs 41
Los Angeles Class 21–27, **22**, **D1** (31), **40**
    cutaway **C** (24–25)
    decommissioning 28–29, 30
    dry deck shelters **44**, **47**
    in dry dock **41**
    rescue operations **42**
    sonar and fire-control systems 34, 39
    surfacing through ice **27**

McNamara, Robert 22
maintenance and repair 40, **41**
mission 5, 40–46
movement control centers 19

Nautilus Class (SSN-571) **A3** (7), 8–10, **8**, **9**, **10**, **37**
Naval Sea Systems Command (NavSea) 21, 22
navigation 8, 35–36
noise analysis 32–35
noise quieting 14–16
North Pole: first vessel to surface at **11**
nuclear fission 6

Office of the Chief of Naval Operations (OpNav) 5
Ohio Class ballistic missile submarines 29
Operation *Desert Storm* (1991) 40–41

paint **9**, **22**
periscopes 18, **D** (31), 32, 36
Permit Class *see* Thresher/Permit Class
Pittsburgh, USS (SSN-720) 40–41
propulsion
    diesel-electric 3–4
    going nuclear 6–8, 10
    nuclear powerplant designation 21
    powerplants with shrouded propulsors 27
    Seawolf Class 27, 28
    shafts **10**
    ship-life reactor cores 30

radar 35
reactor compartments 9, **C** (24–25), **40**
    disposal 46, **46**
rescue operations 42–46, **42**, **G** (45)
Rickover, Admiral Hyman 40

sacrificial anidodes **10**
safety 17, 18–19, 40, 46, **46**
sails
    Los Angeles Class **D** (31), **40**
    in museums 46
    Skipjack Class 12, **16**, **41**
    Sturgeon Class 19, **21**
    Thresher/Permit Class 14, **16–17**, 17–18
    Virginia Class 29
Scamp, USS (SSN-588) **G** (45), **46**
SCB *see* Ship Characteristic Board
Seadragon, USS (SSN-584) 11
SEALs **47**

Seawolf, USS (SSN-575) 10
Seawolf, USS (SSN-705) **27**, 30
Seawolf Class 27–28, **27**, **28**, 30, **D2** (31)
sensors 32–36, **32**
    see also sonar systems
Ship Characteristic Board (SCB) 5, 8
Skate Class **4**, **A4** (7), 10–11, **11**
Skipjack Class 11–13, **B2** (15), **16**, **41**, **G** (45)
snorkel masts **32**
snorkels 4
sonar spheres and domes 9, **22**, 23, **C** (24–25), **29**
sonar systems
    BQG-4 **4**
    BQQ-1 17, 34
    BQQ-3 34
    BQQ-5 17, **34**
    BQR-4 **9**, **9**, 12, 34
    BQR-7 33, **33**
    BQS-6/BQA-3 **32**
    BQS-7 34
    designation 33
    integration with fire-control systems 23
    overview 33–34
    sonar consoles **32**, **33**, **34**
    working method 16
    see also combat-control systems
sound shorts 16
Soviet Union submarines 5, 21, 27, **F** (43)
Spaulding, Petty Officer 46
speed
    and diesel-electric submarines 3–4
    and nuclear submarines 2, 8, 12, 19, 22
Steinel, Sonarman First Class R. E. **32**
stores: loading **5**
Sturgeon Class 3, **B4** (15), 19–20, **21**, 28–29, 34, **F** (43)
    control center 19
SubSafe Program 17, 18–19
surface behaviour 41, 42–44, **44**

Tang Class **4**, 5–6, **A2** (7), 8
Target Motion Analysis (TMA) 34
Tench Class 8
trailing **F** (43)
Thresher, USS (SSN-593) 16–17, 18–19, **32**
Thresher/Permit Class **4**, 14–19, **B3** (15), **17**, 34
time series analysis 33

US Navy
    composition of fast attack submarine fleet 30
    number of submarines 29

Virginia, USS (SSN-774) **29**
Virginia Class 28–30, **29**, **D3** (31), **32**, 36

water supplies 9
weapons
    in action 41
    missile launch tubes 23, **C** (24–25)
    overview 39, **E** (38)
    "smart" torpedoes 32–33
    SubRoc missiles **37**, **E** (38)
    Vertical Launch System (VLS) **40**
Wilkins, Sir Hubert 11

48